PSYCHOLOGY OF THE PLANNED COMMUNITY: THE NEW TOWN EXPERIENCE

Community Psychology Series, Volume 4
American Psychological Association, Division 27

THE COMMUNITY PSYCHOLOGY SERIES
SPONSORED BY
DIVISION 27 OF THE AMERICAN PSYCHOLOGICAL ASSOCIATION
SERIES EDITOR, DANIEL ADELSON, PH.D.

The Community Psychology Series has as its central purpose the building of philosophic, theoretical, scientific and empirical foundations for action research in the community and in its subsystems, and for education and training for such action research.

As a publication of the Division of Community Psychology, the series is particularly concerned with the development of community psychology as a sub-area of psychology. In general, it emphasizes the application and integration of theories and findings from other areas of psychology, and in particular the development of community psychology methods, theories, and principles, as these stem from actual community research and practice.

TITLES IN THE COMMUNITY PSYCHOLOGY SERIES

Volume 1: Man as the Measure: The Crossroads, edited by Daniel Adelson

Volume 2: The University and the Urban Crisis, edited by Howard E. Mitchell

Volume 3: Psychological Stress in the Campus Community: Theory, Research and Action, edited by Bernard L. Bloom

Volume 4: Psychology of the Planned Community: The New Town Experience, edited by Donald C. Klein

PSYCHOLOGY OF THE PLANNED COMMUNITY: THE NEW TOWN EXPERIENCE

Community Psychology Series, Volume 4
American Psychological Association, Division 27

Edited by

Donald C. Klein, Ph.D.

Daniel Adelson,
Series Editor University of California,
San Francisco
John Hopkins University

HUMAN SCIENCES PRESS

72 Fifth Avenue   3 Henrietta Street
NEW YORK, NY 10011 ● LONDON, WC2E 8LU

Library of Congress Catalog Number 77-15502

ISBN: 0-87705-317-0

Copyright © 1978 by Human Sciences Press
72 Fifth Avenue, New York, New York 10011

Printed in the United States of America
89 987654321

Library of Congress Cataloging in Publication Data
Main entry under title:

Psychology of the planned community.

   (Community psychology series ; v. 4)
   1. New towns—Psychological aspects—Addresses, essays, lectures. 2. City planning—Psychological aspects—Addresses, essays, lectures. I. Klein, Donald F., 1928–   II. Series. [DNLM: 1. City planning. 2. Psychology, Social. W1 C0429W no. 4 / HT166 P974]
HT166.P77   301.36'3'019   77-15502
ISBN 0-87705-317-0

Contents

Foreword *by Daniel Adelson*
Preface *by Donald C. Klein*

vii

Foreword

"City air," it has been claimed, "makes free." And through the centuries this has been so, and perhaps even in our time as large cities in America have received those in quest of greater political and psychological freedom— a quest which has led sometimes to expectations and hopes impossibly shut off in dark ghettos. In the city there is anonymity, a multiplicity of communities, and the *freedom to* choose. Yet urban residents have felt the pollution, the lack of community, the violence, the alienation from self and others, and the *freedom from* community and guiding norms more intensely than rural residents.

As knowledge has increased of what is needed to create a community, to make for better schools, and a more healthy and esthetic surrounding, men have sought to apply this knowledge to build "garden cities," to make their homes organically fit the natural surroundings, and to create from the beginning, integrated neighborhoods. They have sometimes succeeded in their goals in part, sometimes in good measure, and sometimes not at all.

For the Master Builder, it appears, has no plan that will fit everyone, nor has he a way of escaping the larger system influences and constraints within which he operates. And more importantly perhaps, in a democratic society, in some ultimate sense, the Master Builder should not make such plans. He can only seek to help create environments which foster individual and community growth in the context of the realities of a particular period and place.

Seen as an experiment, the Columbia experience has much to teach us about the inescapable larger system factors which shape life whether in an old or new town and about the nature of man and his grassroot strivings for self-determination. But it also demonstrates the possibilities of a better transaction between nature and man's physical-social surroundings, and in the questions it raises about the necessary inner and outer conditions for designing and building that better society we are seeking.

D.A.

Preface

When this issue was projected in 1972 the development of comprehensively planned new human settlements (new towns) had become part of America's urban policy. Under the impetus of recently promulgated federal legislation, which authorized loan guarantees and other encouragement to major developers, it was anticipated that scores of new towns and smaller planned unit developments would be created by the year 2,000.

The new towns legislation and subsequent guidelines of the Department of Housing and Urban Development stipulated that comprehensively planned new cities should undertake to provide adequate shelter for diverse economic and racial groups and should install social and technologic innovations that might serve as models for other new and old communities (Department of Housing and Urban Development, 1971).

THE NEW TOWN IDEA

The concept of comprehensively planned total communities within the modern era of rapid transportation and advanced industrial technology is generally believed to have had its origins in the imagination of British reformer Ebenezer Howard in the late 1800's. Howard dreamed, agitated, organized, and worked for the development of so-called garden cities. He envisioned bringing together the best qualities of urban and country living in clusters of modest sized communities linked to one another and to places of employment, culture, and other resources by rapid transit (Howard, 1965).

The new town concept caught hold more rapidly in England and certain European countries than it did in the United States. Comprehensively planned, medium-sized cities have become part of urban policy in Great Britain, France, Holland, and the Scandinavian countries since World War II. In the United States after World War II there were sporadic efforts to design large clusters of dwelling units and related community resources on scale below that of larger cities. Examples of this were Sunny-side Gardens in New York City and Radburn in New Jersey. During the 1930's the federal government sponsored three Greenbelt communities in an effort to demonstrate that urban sprawl could be eliminated with proper planning and enlightened development. Greenbelts were interrupted by World War II and never revived. The three communities were turned over to private interests by 1954.

Reemergence of new towns in this country in the 1960's was largely instigated by private developers, chief among whom were Robert Simon and James Rouse, the practical idealists who conceived of Reston and Columbia, respectively. They attempted to integrate the economics of the capitalist system with the magnificent dream of a total city designed to provide a high quality of life for its citizens. To carry such a dream to fruition, through the stages of design, land acquisition, construction, marketing, and withdrawal of the developer from control of the community, requires a kind of breathtaking practicality which few dreamers possess. Humanitarian goals have a way of bending and sometimes disappearing before the realities of the marketplace, local prejudice, government requirements, and the like. Several of the contributors to this monograph indicate some of the intricacies involved in the interplay between lofty social purpose and economic practicalities. Any attempt of the reader to assess the "success" of the new town dream should keep this interplay in mind.

The new town concept should not be confused with post-World War II massive housing tracts bulldozed out of the landscapes adjacent to major cities throughout the United States. The basic difference lies in the degree of comprehensive planning which seeks to provide most or all of the economic, cultural, and human services provided by a true city. The planning of some new towns—Columbia among them—also sought to create a community that could be more than a single class, uniracial entity. By means of large-scale planning and development, some new community promoters sought to demonstrate that an esthetic, environmentally sound city could be created profitably and at a cost that would not be prohibitive for most Americans.

THE FUTURE OF NEW TOWNS IN THE UNITED STATES

Community reform movements in the United States have had a relatively short and often painful life since World War II. Those that have persisted have done so in only a small proportion of those localities in need of them. Thus the War on Poverty continues as isolated skirmishes in a few communities across the country; Model Cities efforts have lost much of their steam in many places; while local community programs of the much publicized Urban Coalition have ceased to exist. It is painfully possible that the latest version—America's new town movement—may also have proved to be long on promise and short on delivery and sustained effort. In 1974, just as the first drafts of the manuscripts for this monograph were being received, the Republican administration pulled the plug on further underwriting of new towns, and the new town program, already badly hurt by the severe economic recession, virtually ground to a halt.

The future of new towns development remains uncertain. Even under a Democratic administration, comprehensively planned new communities may take a low position on the priority list of social reforms. New towns have been viewed as a mixed blessing by America's more liberal urbanists, many of whom fear that they will divert attention, energy, money, and leadership from the urgent dilemmas of inner cities and the large numbers of ethnic minority persons who live there.

Most new towns enthusiasts do not discount the urgency of problems faced by existing cities. Neither do they view the development of new towns as a solution to the desperate dilemmas of the old. They point instead to the millions of persons who will require new housing in the final 25 years of this century and suggest that existing cities not be asked to bear the entire burden of this need. They further believe that experience gained in developing new towns may, in turn, add knowledge and expertise that can help in dealing with problems of existing localities.

Purposes of the Monograph

Whether or not the new towns movement is reinstated as a significant component of urban policy, there is something to be learned from efforts already underway. This issue is intended to draw forth some of those learnings especially as they pertain to the problems and possibilities for meeting human needs in new localities. It explores certain dynamics of social planning and problem solving in a new environment and, so doing, points to ways in which experience with new town development might contribute to understanding of social problem solving in existing environments.

The issue examines, sometimes acerbically, the utopian possibilities of full-scale communal environments in light of political and economic realities. It should be noted that most of the contributors are psychologists and other applied behavioral scientists who were neither prime movers in the development of new communities nor basic decision-makers who determined the major characteristics of such developments. The inputs of applied behavioral scientists into new community development has been limited at best and nonexistent in most cases. Economic, physical, and political considerations have taken precedence over social concerns. Therefore, it is only fair to point out that certain of the criticisms are offered by people who did not bear the responsibility for the weighty economic, political, land use, marketing, and social decisions which are part of the everyday life of any new town development team.

This issue capitalizes on the fact that Columbia, Maryland, both because of its explicitly stated social goals and its location in the Washington-Baltimore corridor, has attracted an unusually large number of community psychologists and other behavioral scientists who live and, in some cases, do research and other work in the new city. It uses several of these participant-conceptualizers to develop a panoramic view of the growing body of knowledge having to do with institutional development for meeting human needs in new settlements. The hope is that the issue will stimulate community psychologists and related professionals to become interested in new human settlements as an important focus for their research and practice. Concomitantly it is hoped that the monograph will do justice to the knowledge and expertise available within behavioral disciplines that can and should be called on with far greater frequency in the planning and settlement of future new towns as well as in the replanning and rehabilitation of old ones.

HISTORICAL BACKGROUND OF THE MONOGRAPH

My interest in planned communities was awakened when I was a member of a multidisciplinary Core Committee on Community Affairs auspiced by the National

Training Laboratories (NTL)[1] during the 1960's to consider how knowledge of group and organizational behavior and techniques of planned change might be put to use
for community improvement and social problem solving.
Among the many facets explored by the group was that
of the new town, which was represented in the Washington, D.C. area by Reston, Virginia and Columbia. It was
known that the early planning and design of the latter had
been influenced in major ways by a panel of nationally
known social scientists and other human services experts
pulled together by developer James Rouse as an idea-
generating work group (Lemkau, 1969).

Discussion with those responsible for Columbia's institutional development and community management in its
early years kindled my interest to the extent that I persuaded NTL to empower me to establish a branch office
in Columbia which, with cooperation and moral support
from the Rouse Company, might serve as a major center
for NTL's community training, consultation, and research
work both locally and nationwide. The Community Research and Action Laboratory, as it was called, remained
in existence for one year during which it carried out three
major contracts: (1) consultation with top management of
the Columbia Association, the agency responsible for
management of open space, public transportation, and
recreation and human service facilities not provided by
county government; (2) an experimental program with
Antioch College's Columbia branch to teach skills of personal and organizational renewal to advanced under-
graduates; and (3) a project with Johns Hopkins Medical
School's Department of Psychiatry and Behavioral
Science to design a human resource development center
which, via training, consulting, and applied research,
could enhance the delivery and utilization of human services at the state and local level (Klein, 1975, pp. 321–
334).

[1]Subsequently incorporated as NTL Institute for Applied Behavioral
Science.

NTL's Community Research and Action Laboratory (CoRAL) gave way the following year to an equally short-lived Human Resources Center, which grew out of the basic design established in the work with Johns Hopkins Department of Psychiatry. The Center was under the auspices of the Department of Psychiatry and funded by a Drug Abuse Training project of the state's Drug Abuse Administration. Administrative and financial problems led to the abandonment of the Center once the drug contract was completed.

Despite the demise of both attempts to develop ongoing resource centers for community problem solving, the efforts left the new town with an unusually large concentration of resourceful community psychologists and other behavioral scientists who had been attracted to the community either as staff members of the ill-fated organizations or because of the existence of a group of like-minded colleagues who made the new town an attractive, challenging place in which to settle or work. The presence of this group has contributed to efforts to identify and respond to human service needs of Columbia's residents, some of which are described in the monograph.

To maintain colleagueship beyond the time when the Human Resources Center ceased to exist, the group established another version of the Community Research and Action Laboratory (CoRAL II). It is an independent, non-profit organizational and community consultation, training, and research agency that continues to serve as a focal point for applied research activities as well as a base for individual members' training and consulting work. CoRAL II has carried forward in a modest fashion the original concept of the NTL project, which was to provide an innovative research and development center for an entire community that would facilitate leadership emergence, problem solving, and the development of resources for a self-helping community within the rapidly growing new town and the surrounding region. The youth research reported in the monograph was conducted under CoRAL II auspices and the monograph itself was made possible because the Laboratory served as a personal and financial support base.

ORGANIZATION OF THIS ISSUE

The issue consists of four sections:

I.   New Habitats: Dreams and Realities
II. The New Town as a Laboratory of Human Relations: the Case of Columbia, Maryland
III. The Community Psychologist as Citizen and Practitioner in New Community Settings
IV. Point-Counterpoint: Perspectives on New Community Realities

Section I introduces the reader to the history and philosophy of the new towns movement and gives special emphasis to the basic social, economic, and political considerations which have interwoven to form the texture of the movement in the United States. It includes a description of an attempt to make the development of new towns relevant to the interlinked problems of racism and economic barriers faced by many Americans. The Section closes with a description by a community psychologist of how he combed the field of psychology to discover knowledge and insights that could be applied to the design of a hypothetical new town.

Section II takes the reader to Columbia, the new town which in 1967 began to take shape on seventeen thousand acres of rolling farm land about midway between Baltimore and Washington, D.C. Columbia's unique social philosophy and the fact that social science consultants were involved early in its design has excited the interest and attention of many applied behavioral scientists, among whom are several community psychologists whose contributions are included in this issue. Each planned community is potentially an exciting case study in community development. Section II treats Columbia as such a case study by presenting facets of its development and its social institutions.

Section III presents the experiences and reflections of psychologists who have used their psychological know-how both as workers and residents in new towns. A husband-wife team describes how they went about helping to develop a sense of community within one of Columbia's residential enclaves. In the second paper a psychologist describes how she developed community consulting and planning skills on the job and in the process became a social engineer of innovative community change projects.

Section IV closes this issue with three quite different reflections on the psychology of the new town experience as it is reflected in the first three sections and especially in those contributions having to do with the Columbia case. A noted community sociologist shares his reactions to those contributions and comments on the similarities and differences between new towns and established communities. The first manager of Columbia, who was himself intimately involved in the planning and development process for the new town, addresses himself to the thorny questions which must be raised when anyone asks, "Did the new town work?" Finally, I have taken the opportunity to comment on the question of what psychology and the applied behavioral sciences have to offer at this time to planners and developers of new communities.

REFERENCES

Department of Housing and Urban Development. *Draft Regulations for Urban Growth and New Community Development Act of 1970.* Washington, D.C.: Federal Register, 36 F.R. 14205-14, 1971.

Howard, E. *Garden cities of tomorrow.* Cambridge, Mass.: MIT Press Paperback Edition, 1965.

Klein, D. Developing human services in new communities, a separate of vol. II. In H. Schulberg & F. Baker (Eds.), *Developments in human services.* New York: Behavioral Publications, 1975.

Lemkau, P. The planning project for Columbia. In M. Schore and F. Mannino (Eds.), *Mental health and the community.* New York: Behavioral Publications, 1969.

Section I

NEW HABITATS: DREAMS AND REALITIES

1. Introduction

Section I is designed to set a contextual framework for the remainder of this issue. It introduces the historical, social, and philosophical origins of the new town movement and ends with two papers which present, respectively, the two very different perspectives on new town development of a civil rights activist turned new community builder, and of a community psychologist who has had the opportunity to be a central figure in a team charged with the design of a hypothetical new community.

James A. Clapp, Director of a graduate program in city planning at San Diego State University, has in a very few pages set forth the highlights of mankind's urban inventiveness. His article ranges from archeological findings indicating that the deliberate and purposeful design of settlements may be at least 7,000 years old to a quick review of the various purposes to which new town development has been put in Europe and the United States.

Royce Hanson, a political scientist and planner, examines the utopian aims of the contemporary new town movement with an eye to the practical problems involved in trying to achieve those aims in the context of modern social and political realities. His contribution has two basic themes: (1) the new town is less of a physical reality than it is, in essence, an expression of a social theory of the metropolis; (2) the concept of the new town as a comprehensive approach to urban reform, however compelling and persistent, proves to be exquisitely fragile when exposed to the pressures and constraints of modern America. He concludes that they will succeed in this country only when the federal government wholeheartedly joins its financial and technical resources to those of the private developer in order to nurture the earliest stages of the new community's physical and social development.

Floyd B. McKissick, the former Director of the Congress of Racial Equality (CORE) and a civil rights leader of the 1960's, has turned his attention to the challenge of developing a planned multi-racial community under black leadership on thousands of acres of old plantation land in North Carolina. One of the few communities awarded a loan guarantee by the Department of Housing and Urban Development, Soul City has at its essence the conviction that in our society "social goals are inseparable from economic power." In his paper for this issue, McKissick shares his dream of a nonracist, economically viable community. He also sets forth some of the practical problems which must be faced in the areas of marketing, finance, economic modeling, environmental design, and land use. Finally, he sketches mechanisms that have been created in order to foster the economic development of Soul City and its surroundings, which in his view is essential if social dreams are to become communal realities.

Stanley A. Murrell, a community psychologist on the faculty of the University of Louisville, concludes Section I with a fascinating account of the approaches he used when given the opportunity to apply psychology to the planning of a comprehensive new community. Murrell comes as close as any psychologist has to serving at the core of a new community design process. Associated with the Urban Studies Center at the University of Louisville, he and a team of architects and physical planners took on the task of designing the model for a new community that could serve as a relocation center for rural poor families migrating to medium-sized metropolitan communities. Though NewCom as a totality has never been built—and may never be—it has been used as a model for various aspects of other community developments elsewhere in the United States. It is in a way an expression of what Hanson meant when he wrote about the compelling nature of the new town concept as a model for problem solving as distinct from an easily realizable comprehensive design.

The word "utopia" comes up again and again in this Section. This is to be expected because new towns are exercises in bringing to fruition what many consider to be impossible dreams. Among the hopes and aspirations alluded to in Section I are the restructuring of urban life; achieving a more perfect harmony between nature and technology; dealing with the modern metropolis as a whole system and in holistic terms; building a community without racism; and optimizing the match between the needs and preferences of individuals and the positive reinforcers of the community as environment.

Developers of new communities must think big, at least when considered from the perspective of the psychologist whose idea of humanity in the mass is most typically restricted to the complexities of a face-to-face group, an organization, or occasionally, a more complex institution (e.g., a school system), or a set of institutions (e.g., the criminal justice system). When new town developers think of scale they take into account millions of dollars expended before income even begins to trickle in, land use embracing thousands of acres (Columbia's land mass is greater than that of Manhattan Island), and projected populations ranging from 50,000 to upwards of 400,000 people (e.g., Irvine, California.) They hold that great economic and social benefits can be reaped from planning and building on a massive scale and with sufficient population density to permit diversity of resources and the investment in such expensive necessities as public transportation. To realize profit and to achieve the desired public benefits they must invest large amounts of money and long hard years of work on ventures that in many respects exceed the complexities and uncertainties of putting human beings on the moon.

The new town developer's psychology must be the very opposite of paranoia. It is a condition for which we in psychology have no suitable term. The condition consists of projecting a realistic vision on to the environment together with a basic assumption of benevolent opportunity. The assumption holds that if something really needs to be done—even something as complex and risky as creating a new city—it can somehow be managed. A corollary assumption is that the vast majority of people will respond affirmatively to opportunities to invest their efforts and energies in projects designed to achieve specific goals of social betterment that any reasonable person can readily see are logical and necessary.

New town advocates, as the papers in Section I indicate, are more apt to be practical idealists than utopian dreamers. They are very much in touch with the realities, inherent complexities, and potential adversities of their quests. Hanson devotes a major portion of his paper to the "hard realities" faced by private entrepreneurs of new towns in the United States. McKissick's contribution reflects the realization that dreams of two-way integration must make their way through the racist residues of the majority white society, and that integration exists alongside other considerations, such as marketing, financial, economic, environmental, and others. Murrell, in turn, begins with the recognition of factors bound to buffet any new town during its planning and implementation. In the eyes of some of his colleagues in psychology, Murrell may well be seen as the most utopian member of the contributors to Section I. He has undertaken the novel task of demonstrating that the raw material of psychological knowledge and insights is applicable to strengthening the physical and social designs of a new community. Some may question whether the microcosmic inquiries of contemporary psychology are, in fact, relevant to the macrocosmic undertaking of designing an entire city. In any event, it is the only psychology we have at the moment and Murrell has taken the courageous step of laying it on the line in a way that appears to combine practicality with idealism.

This issue of the *Community Psychology Series* makes the assumption that community psychology is, or can become, far more than the practice of psychology in a community setting. It includes the study of and attempts to shape the *psychology of the community.* Section I begins the process of describing the framework of political and social considerations within which the psychology of community-building on a macrosystemic scale takes place. The reader is greeted by concepts and assumptions which, though unfamiliar to most community psychologists let alone to psychologists generally, are by now deeply embedded in the multidisciplinary field of urban design. Though not generally treated by community psychologists, these ideas lie at the core of an understanding of that incredibly complicated human invention we refer to glibly as "community."

2. New Towns from Past to Present: An Historical Sketch

JAMES A. CLAPP

More than a few students of history consider the city to be man's greatest and most complex invention. Indeed, in any discussion of civilization the city appears so consistent and pervasive a backdrop as to be at times taken for granted. A good deal of debate rages over the origins of the first cities, and what essential locations or environmental and social conditions played a role. We know that there must be reasons why cities happened into history, but their first appearance reaches so far back into proto-history as to obscure their causes. Archeologists continue to dig for the answers while the rest of us attempt to grapple with the problems and adjust to the realities of present-day urban life. However they came about, cities are now a fact of life.

Nevertheless, there is evidence dating quite deep into history that men have attempted to employ the urban invention in deliberate and purposeful ways. Interestingly, these conscious uses of purposeful city-founding may retain a valuable function some 6,000 years after their appearance. Cities did not happen in an ecological sense—the way foliage seeks out water courses. The first basic purposes of cities may have been crudely simple: to remain near a mystical place; to provide for safety in numbers; or to provide a settlement where the hunting, fishing, or farming were good. But whatever these original purposes may have been, there is some evidence from urban antiquity of the deliberate establishment of settlements for predetermined and more specific purposes and necessities. Wall paintings in ancient Catal Huyuk (circa 6,200 B.C.) show a rectilinear street pattern, hinting that the design of the settlement may have preceded its construction (Hamblin, 1973, pp. 46–47). Nearby sources of obsidian may explain the selection of its site. However, stronger evidence of town-founding for specific purposes comes from Egypt where some new towns were established to house slaves and artisans engaged in pyramid construction (U.S. National Resources Committee, 1939, p. 12).

The Greeks are reputed to have founded the first new towns for special purposes in Europe (Stewart, 1952, p. 14). The Greek new towns began some 3,000 years ago for the purposes of colonization, commerce, and the absorption of population increases in the city-states. This last purpose was necessitated by the limits of food and water supply (Gallion & Eisner, 1960, p. 19). New towns were termed "neopoli," many of which remain viable today. Likewise, the Macedonians and Romans made extensive use of the new towns concept, principally for purposes of military strategy and the settlement of newly acquired territories. It is estimated that there were some 60 new towns founded during the Macedonian period (16 of which were named after Alexander the Great)(U.S. National Resources Committee, 1939, pp. 12–13). The Romans further refined and systematized the process of new town construction, evolving the Greek, Hippodamus' grid pattern of street construction into the Roman "insulae," or block pattern, which was characteristic of all Roman "castra." While many of these towns were designed originally for limited populations, a number evolved subsequently into major world cities, notably London and Paris (Stewart, 1952, pp. 18–19).

The Dark Ages that followed the decline of Rome marked a slowing of the founding of new towns. However, as strong rulers began gradually to reappear, so also did the founding of new towns, particularly in Germany ("neustadts" such as Aachen), in France ("villenueves" such as Montpazier), and in England.

The Renaissance proved more to be a period of expansion of existing cities and towns rather than new towns building. However, consistent with the fact that the period was one of a generation of new ideas as well as jostling among emerging imperial powers and city-states, more attention was given to concepts of new town construction and location related to both fortified towns (Scamozzi and Da Vinci) and idealistic forms of settlements (U.S. National Resources Committee, 1939, p. 15). Second, this period was marked by greater exploration, in particular into the New World, which set the scene once again for the employment of the new towns concept in conjunction with colonialization of new territories.

Early settlements in America assumed many of the features of the European new towns. The gridiron pattern was most dominant, but in some cases the radial pattern was employed, either alone or in conjunction with the grid pattern. Some of the best known examples of early American new towns are Williamsburg, Annapolis, Savannah, and New Orleans. During the colonial expansion and up to the Revolution, the building of new towns continued in gradually acquired territories. Of particular interest with regard to its design and purpose is Washington, D.C. After much deliberation, the Founding Fathers selected the Potomac site in order to avoid the commercial environment of many already established cities. Its grand design and scale, which were originally determined by Pierre L'Enfant (a protegé of Hausmann, the planner of Paris), and later revised by Andrew Ellicott, appealed to aristocratic tastes and promised to rival its European counterparts (Feiss, 1960, p. 86).

INDUSTRIALIZATION AND THE MODERN NEW TOWNS MOVEMENT

What has been described as the "new towns movement" had its beginnings with the emergence of urban industrialism during the 19th Century. No attempt will be made here to summarize the sweeping social and economic changes that were visited upon cities during this period, except that the new towns movement, like the city planning movement of which it is a part, had its roots in the period of reform that arose in reaction to the physical, social, and economic conditions of the late 19th Century city.

The origins of the new towns movement can be traced to the writings of many of the 19th Century reformers, but as Rodwin (1956) points out, " . . . the notion of recasting our urban environment in the form of garden cities owes its contemporary formulation to Ebenezer Howard [p. 9]." What made Howard (1850–1928) the progenitor of the new towns movement and distinguished him from many other social reformers of his time was his pragmatism. He not only set down his ideas in some detail, but promoted them actively through the establishment of the Garden Cities Association and later in the promotion of the new towns of Letchworth and Welwyn.

The Garden City idea was simple, but inspirational for its time. In his influential book, *Garden Cities of Tomorrow*, Ebenezer (1965) argued for the "marriage of town and country" in the development of completely new communities. Rather than concentrate upon specifications for the physical layout of his Garden City idea, which he chose to express only in schematic form, Howard chose to emphasize the social and economic features of this notion. He insisted that such towns should be of limited population (around 30,000 residents) and that they should be physically delimited by a surrounding "greenbelt," and that other features should include such social facilities as "convalescent homes" and "farms for epileptics." But the central theme of Howard's book focuses on the economics of the Garden City scheme. As he summarized it:

> The economies with which we have dealt are, it will be seen, effected by the two simple expedients we have referred to. First, by buying the land *before* a new value is given to it by migration, the migrating people obtain a site at an extememly low figure, and secure the coming increment for themselves and those who come after them; and secondly, by coming to a new site, they do not have to pay large sums for old building, for compensation for disturbance, and for heavy legal charges [p. 75].

It is the capture of this very increment in value created by new migrants to the new town that is the fundamental economic inspiration for the privately constructed new town in the United States today. Of course Howard envisioned this increment to benefit the entire community; in the privately constructed new town this increment comprises the profit margin of the entrepreneur.

The widespread appeal of Howard's ideas is witnessed by the fact that by 1913 there were Garden Cities associations in seven countries and an international federation promoting the development of new towns. Examples of the strongest influence of the Garden City idea are found in Great Britain. Although the air attacks of World War II and the postwar shortages of building materials (as well as the postwar victory of the Labor Party) had much to do with the passage of the Town and Country Planning Act of 1946 which contained the mechanism for the construction of new towns Howard's influence upon planning ideas certainly played an important conceptual role. Since 1946 Britain has constructed and designated sites for several new towns. By 1962 eight new towns were underway in the London region for the purpose of providing for population overspill, and another seven were underway in other parts of the country for the purposes of both population overspill and regional development.

The Soviet Union has reputedly founded more than 800 new settlements since 1926, of which about one-third were situated in totally undeveloped areas. Russian new towns have been developed for a variety of purposes, generally as part of broad schemes for national development and the decentralization of industry. Many of the earlier towns were associated with extractive industries and later expanded for the development of manufacturing (Shkvarikov, Haucke, & Smirnova, 1964).

The necessities for decentralizing population and accommodating large increases in population from immigration formed the rationale for Israel's new towns program. Originally some 30 new towns were planned to serve as regional centers for the Kibbutzim, although the number was later reduced considerably because of difficulties in decentralizing industry. Ashdod, the largest, was established as a new port to relieve the pressures on Haifa (Silkin, 1967).

New towns in the highly urbanized Netherlands have been intended mostly to provide relief from population pressures on major urban centers. However more recent developments have been intended to spread new growth into less developed areas and reclaimed polders.

Other countries in which several new towns are under construction or have been completed are:

Canada: mostly single enterprise new communities built by industries associated with mining and production of paper and aluminum. One of the better known examples is Kitimat, B.C., founded by the Aluminum Company of Canada.

Germany: several industrial new towns associated with heavy industry and automobile production industries.

France: concentration on planned extensions of existing communities and several large new towns in the
Paris region and other nearby large cities.

South Africa: several new towns associated with gold-
mining, industry, and chemicals.

Sweden: new towns built in association with mining
and industry, and the renowned planned satellites
around Stockholm.

NEW TOWNS IN AMERICA

New towns in the United States may be classified under
three types of sponsorship: Industrial, Governmental, and
other Private Enterprise Communities. However these
forms of sponsorship may well become integrated in the
development of a given new town (U.S. National Resources Committee, 1939). The new towns of industrial
enterprises are varied. Some were originated as single-
industry towns; others have attracted several industrial
tenants. However, in many industrial towns the types of
industries tended to be associated with resource extrac-
tion and hence were more resource- than market oriented in their locations. While a number were strictly
"company towns," other industries found that well-
planned communities could function as a valuable fringe
benefit in attracting other enterprises and employees.

Although only in recent years has the United States
established a program involving government assistance
for the development of new towns, there are a number of
examples of new towns that were constructed in association with specific governmental activities. The major governmental   purposes   that   have   resulted   in   the
development of government-sponsored new towns have
been in connection with wartime industry and housing
(Brooklawn N.J.; Cradock and Hilton, Va.; and Fairlawn,
N.J.), strategic operations (Oak Ridge, Tenn.; Los Alamos,
N.M.; and Richland, Wash.), and regional resource devel-

opment (Norris, Tenn. and Boulder City, Nev.). Others, in particular the Greenbelt Towns of the Suburban Resettlement Administration, are connected with employment generation and planning demonstration projects. The planning of the Greenbelt Towns (Greenbelt, Md.; Greendale, Wis.; and Greenhills, Ohio) was based on the application of three principles: the Garden City idea of a community within a greenbelt, the Radburn idea of the use of the "superblock," and the "neighborhood unit" principle. Along with Radburn, N.J., they remain today as the most faithful application of the physical planning principles of Howard and his disciples (Mumford, 1941, p. 2).

In recent years the interests of students of the new towns concept has been stimulated by a new chapter in the history of American new town development, characterized by the advent of the large-scale developer and the renewed interest of large industrial corporations in the financial and experimental advantages of new towns. Large increases in population growth after World War II, higher incomes, increased mobility, the interstate highway program, government support of home ownership, and a general expansion of credit appear to be the principal underlying factors in this trend. Although a few postwar private developments like the Levittowns and Park Forest are examples of this phase of new town construction, the major period of activity has been in the 1960's. In 1964 Robert Murray, one observer of the trend, remarked that:

> Across the U.S. there are at least 75 completely planned communities of 1,000 or more acres where developers are creating facilities to house more than 6 million people. And by 1985 when these new towns should be completed, their aggregate built up value will probably exceed $75 billion . . . equal to more than three years total U.S. housing production. Yet these big new communities are in or on the edge of metropolitan areas, most particularly in the areas of greatest population growth [p. 123].

The inauguration of such a significant number of new town projects was an outgrowth of the fact that an increasing number of large-scale developers recognized that total community development, as opposed to strictly residential development, offered considerable potential for profits that would accrue from the higher land values created by residential development. The subsequent development and property sale for commercial and industrial areas demanded by large-scale residential development appears to be one of the central aspects of commercial interest in new town development in the U.S. This interest has been expressed not only by the traditional private development sector of the economy engaged in residential development, but also by nontraditional but highly capitalized sectors of private enterprise such as oil companies and industries associated with construction materials. Such large corporations have proved better able to sustain the extremely high front-end costs associated with development of new towns, and in the case of oil companies, have previously purchased large land-holdings (Clapp, 1971a, Ch. 5).

Although urban planners had for many years extolled the virtues of new towns and called for legislation and public policies to encourage their creation, the advent of a large amount of private activity in new town construction appears largely responsible for the passage of a moderately scaled new towns program by the federal government in 1966 (Clapp, 1971a, Ch. 6). The potential advantages of the new town concept as a solution to a variety of urban development problems is indicated by the fact that the new town concept has been offered as a means for controlling urban sprawl, alleviating transportation problems, preserving open space, revitalizing both inner-city areas and depressed rural regions, and deconcentrating populations for civil defense purposes (Clapp, 1971, Ch. 4).

Whether the current American new towns such as Columbia, Md.; Reston, Va.; Irvine, Ca.; Litchfield Park, Ariz.; Jonathan, Minn.; Lysander, N.Y.; Soul City, N.C.;

and numerous others will deliver on some of these promises of the new towns concept remains to be determined. At present these communities range in purpose and planning from minor departures from conventional real estate development practices to cautious experimentation. But as yet governmental role in American new town development is currently minimal and lacking in mechanisms to provide firm direction over location, planning, and social and governmental factors (Clapp, 1971b).

What is evident however, is the remarkable resiliency and flexibility of the new town concept from ancient times to the present. It encompasses the notions of deliberate town building to achieve predetermined social purposes, preplanning, limited size, and strong controls over the timing and phasing of development. As such it will probably continue to function as a magnet for innovative notions in physical and social planning and design and offer on-going refinement of the urban invention to meet secular urban problems and necessities.

REFERENCES

Clapp, J. *New towns and urban policy.* New York: Dunellen, 1971. (a)

Clapp, J. Potentially 'counter-intuitive' elements in federal new communities legislation, *University of San Diego Law Review,* 1971, *9* 73–82. (b)

Feiss, C. New towns for America. *Journal of the American Institute of Architects,* 1960, *33* (1), 1960.

Gallion, A. & Eisner, S. *The urban pattern.* Princeton: Van Nostrand, 1960.

Hamblin, D. & the Editors of Time-Life Books. *The first cities.* New York: Time-Life Books, 1973.

Howard, E. *Garden cities of tomorrow.* (3rd ed.) Cambridge: M.I.T. Press, 1965.

Mumford, L. Introduction. In O. Fulmer, *Greenbelt* Washington, D.C.: American Council on Public Affairs, 1941.

Murray, R. New towns for America. *House and Home,* 1964, *25* (2), 123.

Rodwin, L. *The British new towns policy.* Cambridge: Harvard University Press, 1956.

Shkvarikov, V., Haucke, M., & Smirnova, O. The building of new towns in the USSR. *Ekistics,* 1964, *17* (108), 307.

Silkin, L. Israel's new town programme. *Town and Country Planning,* 1967, *35* (3), 146–147.

Stewart, C. *A prospect of cities.* London: Longmans-Green, 1952.

United States National Resources Committee. *Urban planning and land policies, part II of the supplementary report of the urbanism committee of the national resources committee.* Washington, D.C.: U.S. Government Printing Office, 1939.

3. New Towns: Utopian Prospects—Hard Realities

ROYCE HANSON

At its core, the new town movement is a moral and social crusade to improve the urban condition. Its origins are in social reform and its objectives are to restructure urban form and life to achieve a more perfect harmony among nature, technology, and economic and social classes. Its most ardent proponents have been people of immense social conscience and evangelic force: Ebenezer Howard, Louis Mumford, Louis Wright, Heikie Von Hertzen, Robert E. Simon, and James Rouse.[1]

To the extent that any real reform of social institutions is utopian, the new towns movement may be so classified. It is also, however, a practiced art, and susceptible to empirical as well as logical proofs. While today's proponents do not claim new towns are the panacea envisioned by Ebenezer Howard, they believe that new towns have proved themselves to be better human environments than other forms of urban development and a far more practical approach to the problems of urban society than most others. New towns, as envisioned by the movement's

[1]An historical review of the contemporary new towns movement can be found in *New Towns and Urban Policy* by James Clapp (1971). The reader is also referred to Ebenezer Howard's original treatise on the concept of the "garden city" (Howard, 1965).

prophets, are in fact the only comprehensive approach to urban reform that has been offered by modern social philosophers. To some fair extent, the shortcomings of those that have been built can also be laid not to the ideas and ideals of the movement, but to the extent to which those concepts have been vitiated by their builders or governments.

The resilience of the new towns idea is demonstrated by the perseverance of the faithful who stood with Howard until Welwyn was built and by those disciples who established the Town and Country Planning Association and were ready with new towns legislation in Great Britain after World War II. In America the depression left Radburn an unfinished but highly evocative contribution to town planning. The aborted efforts of the Greenbelt towns also linked the frontier utopianism of settlements like New Harmony and industrial utopias such as Pullman with postwar urban thought in America.

As an utopian idea, new towns begin with Howard in the late 1800's. The earlier utopian settlements and industrial towns should be distinguished as utopias of a different sort, based largely on a working out of religious or industrial salvation. A most unique utopian concept of the new towns movement initiated by Howard is that of so restructuring the institutions of urban development that all the simpler ideals of community life and reconciliation of urban technology and economics with nature could be achieved.

The ideas that man needs community and communal identity, that he should democratically govern himself and share in the wealth and power he generates are hardly novel. A new town seeks to achieve these and other objectives, such as human scale of settlements, social and economic balance, harmony of urban development with nature and agriculture, and social betterment, through a new system of development.

While the movement's ideas have sometimes been held captive to physical determinists, new towns, at root, are not physical but social theories of the metropolis. The new towns idea seeks to do no less than view the modern metropolis as a whole system, and to deal with it in holistic terms. It is this central idea which is most utopian and least grasped, and it is failure to grasp this central reality that leads to so many new towns falling short of their theoretical potential.

Urbanization involves many institutions and processes. An institution is simply a systematic pattern of behavior. Urban development institutions include industries, bureaucracies, legal and regulatory systems, financial organizations, social processes and technical systems and disciplines as well as various human and natural ecological systems. Cities and metropolises are somewhat chaotic because there is little political and social agreement on what they should be. The only apparent agreement is not to follow any simple, clear path. The result is a system of economic and legal institutions that specialize in parts and govern only at the conflict points by arbitrating disputes or regulating obvious abuses, but do not provide clear, coherent, or comprehensive direction.

In part, the problem of the modern metropolis is its complexity, which is not only different in scale but in kind from the days when the new towns idea was born to address the evils of the industrial city. Urban population growth alone has accelerated so rapidly that forms of development which acquire strong control over land absorption cannot even be invented and used in time to deal with the problems for which they were designed. The great transformation of agriculture from labor intensive to capital inclusive enterprise, combined with the rise of the post-industrial city stimulated the pace of urbanization in the last half century. As recently as the New Deal era, demographers were expecting the nation to still be half rural by the mid-1970's. The rise of the automobile as an institution of social and economic life also transformed the city and the home-work-community relationship. What the auto began, mass communication has augmented so that community has taken on entirely different proportions than it had only a generation ago.

The rush of events and the rapid ossification of some of these crucial urban institutions combines with the sluggish movement of others to frustrate the use of a new towns strategy of urban reform. Note, for instance, that some of the outstandingly successful European new towns, such as Tapiola and the Stockholm satellites, are built in areas where they could absorb a far higher percentage of new growth than the cases of Reston, Columbia, Jonathan, etc. in the U.S. The importance of this lies in the amount of time required to plan, design, and build a single new town, let alone a whole galaxy of them for a single metropolis.

This problem is closely related to the institutions of physical development, of which finance is vital. Land acquisition on a grand scale is both costly and time consuming. The celebrated problem of front-end costs—land holding, taxes, interest, and infrastructure—present formidable difficulties resulting in long delays before a positive cash flow is possible in a single development, let alone a series of concurrent developments. The result has been that most ventures in the U.S. have been seriously undercapitalized from the start.

Some of these problems could be overcome by larger and more concentrated Public participation. But government participation in development is also institutionalized to avoid the sine qua non of effective new town development: favoritism to the new towns over all other forms of urbanization. Thus, few local jurisdictions will forestall investment in other types of communities, even if they retard or complicate the new town. The result is that the utopian ideal of living and working in the new town is only marginally achieved, because the early states of growth depend on residential settlement of people already holding jobs elsewhere in the area. It will probably take about 30 to 50 years for new towns now being built to more fully realize this objective. Similarly, the multiclass objective of new towns falls short in the face of the need to maintain a reasonable cash flow, best obtained by providing earlier emphasis on higher priced properties. This natural marketing problem is, of course, exacerbated when the U.S. government welches on its commitments to subsidized housing.

The exclusive reliance on private industry to build new towns in the U.S. is also bound to diminish the movement; private profit is not always compatible with social benefits. This reliance also leads to the tendency for new towns to be viewed simply as large-scale urban developments, merely an extension of subdivision activity. This rigid thinking is somewhat reflected in the 1970 Housing Act, but especially the administration of the Act, which insists on dealing with new *communities;* not *new towns* (Howes, 1970). The difference is not merely semantic, but establishes in both government and industry a different psychology from, for example, that which was dominant in the British new towns program.

In the modern political market, ideas are short-lived. The exigencies of Office of Management and Budget and Congressional oversight demand annual appropriations and accountability. The insatiable demand for new "solutions" to be embalmed into new legislative proposals tends to dissipate a great deal of creative energy that might well be used to sustain programs such as new towns. There is also the problem that new towns are a systemic and comprehensive concept, buried in a highly specialized bureaucracy. They take a long time to plan, let alone complete. In an age of instant gratification they are born failures, as they cannot come to fruition during the terms of an incumbent administration. Our political institutions, thus, are not geared to make the commitments required for new town development. Awash with social change, they scurry to respond, or to *appear* responsive, *today.* A new town strongly endorsed by one government may be reviled by its successor. Where zoning and public works are essential to a schedule of development, such shifts in policy can be fatal.

The inertia of going concerns complicates achievement

of the promise of new towns. School systems, for instance, are crucial elements in the new town philosophy, which seeks to utilize education as a means of building community and of benefiting residents. Indeed, the new town provides an environment and a philosophy in which educational systems can be "remade"—except for the fact that state and local school policies generally inhibit extensive organizational or pedagogic experimentation or change.

Health care institutions are, if anything, more rigid. Medical societies, hospitals, and insurance carriers operate under formal and rigid rules that are hard to adjust so that a new town may have a better system of health care than other communities. Religious groups, while often open to new approaches to worship and communion, have both clerical and lay governments to appease. Moreover, those who come to live in new towns are only changing residence, not personalities or beliefs. They still cling to their prior group affiliations, many of which are far stronger influences on their behavior than the new environment in which they may merely reside.

All the things I have mentioned are far more complex than in Howard's time, or even in the late 1940's when the British new towns were being started. The interlocking of investments, institutions, and computers has left much less latitude for dramatic changes in the way we do things. Put perhaps too simply, experiments are not mortgageable.

In the face of the great inertia of urban institutions, the new social processes of new towns are extremely frail. Surely, if the physical development of new towns requires "front-end" participation by government just to allow survival, their social development requires it even more. Otherwise, the "too little too early" approach of Housing and Urban Development dooms them. Especially in the first generation of new town growth—say the first 15 to 20 years—there is no indigenous system of life support institutions, there is no civic history, no set of lasting voluntary institutions to bind the new town together. These things will all develop but they take time.

What we have learned from our flirtation with the new town utopias is that the serious determination of the public or private developer to provide a better place for a better way of urban life is a necessary but hardly a sufficient force. We have also been learning the hard way that utopias are not built quickly or cheaply and maybe not at a profit. We should also be learning that an idea as compelling as that of new towns will not disappear so long as people have the capacity to believe that they can solve problems, even as complex as those confronting the metropolis.

As to other more fragmentary approaches to dealing with urban problems, such as increased emphasis on law enforcement, affirmative action in employment, and special education programs for the disadvantaged, they are consistently working less well than before, but we are doing them better than ever. In times like these, as Adlai Stevenson once remarked, someone always cries out for "practical" men, and unfortunately, there always seem to be plenty of them around.

REFERENCES

Clapp, J. *New towns and urban policy.* New York: Dunellen, 1971.

Howard, E. *Garden cities of tomorrow.* Cambridge: M.I.T. Press, 1965 (3rd ed.) (Originally published in 1898 as *To-morrow: a Peaceful Path to Real Reform.*)

Howes, J. The shape of federal involvement in new community building—1970. In S. Weiss, E. Kaiser, & R. Burby (Eds.), *New community development: planning process, implementation, and emerging social concerns.* (Vol. 2) Chapel Hill, N.C.: Center for Urban and Regional Studies, U. of North Carolina at Chapel Hill, 1971.

4. Social Dreams and Realities of Soul City

FLOYD B. MCKISSICK

The civil rights movement of the 1960's was a partially successful attempt to change society. It will take full and total integration to abolish racism, but this has not even been tried, much less accomplished. However, we have learned our lesson well: social goals are inseparable from economic power. The civil rights movement has evolved in the 1970's as an economic rights movement.

There are two basic approaches to integration, whether economic or social. The first approach, and the one most widely attempted, features whites responding to the numerous pressures of a society awakening gradually to the imperfections of its past. They ask blacks to come join them, to "integrate." It is a little more difficult for most whites to consider doing the integrating themselves, with a black initiator-leader-dreamer, inviting them to become part of a process they do not control. But that is the Soul City dream—to build a community where blacks have taken the initiative and will be the primary developers, but can also invite members of any other race to come share in the adventure. The question remains, of course, whether America is ready to allow a black to dream an equal dream, perhaps even to help see it through to fruition. The Soul City new town project is designed to show that blacks can. Soul City, incidentally, has been integrated from its inception. Gordon R. Carey, a former jailmate of mine, a colleague at CORE, and now the Soul City Company's Secretary and Treasurer, is the white dreamer who has been living and working and sweating it out down at the Soul City site since 1969.

Soul City is located in Warren County, North Carolina. The area is sparsely populated, with blacks comprising around 60 percent, Indians 3 percent, and whites the remainder of the residents. The present towns are majority white, with the blacks and Indians living in the countryside. If we anticipate that the population of Soul City will approximate that of the county at large with blacks in the majority, a sizeable white minority, and a smaller number of Indians, both black and white will be offered a unique living situation. Blacks will be able to live in a community envisioned, planned, and developed primarily by members of their own race. They will be participating in the decision-making process in the community from its inception. Instead of fighting for that right, and considering it an accomplishment when one or two representatives achieve it, we will have a community where that right is assumed. On the other hand, whites will be offered the unprecedented opportunity of living in a vibrant new community where they may be the minority, not in a "slumming" or "radical chic" atmosphere, but as an integral part of the community and, until the end of this century, working side-by-side with blacks to make Soul City a reality.

My personal interest in the new town concept stems from my experiences in World War II. After the devastation of the war, the United States government stepped in to help the Europeans rebuild their cities from the rubble up. The new communities program in the Department of Housing and Urban Development was fashioned by Congress to offer similar aid to those who were willing to build new towns in this country as an alternative to the unplanned, often chaotic, urban growth of the past. In addition to the advantages of planned physical development, the new town concept also offers the developer the opportunity of planning for social development. However, I doubt that there could be more effective means of bringing a new city dreamer back to earth than by having him apply for a commitment from the United States Department of Housing and Urban Development, New Communities Administration. Once a developer has had to contend for months with marketing feasibility studies, financial feasibility studies, economic models, environmental studies, multi-year land-use planning studies, *ad infinitum*, he has to have a fairly realistic appreciation of the possibilities and the limitations of new towns as a vehicle for social change.

One of our earliest articulated goals for Soul City was to reverse the tide of emigration which has plagued the South, and especially its minority and rural population for so many years. For the first years of our development, we will continue to try to serve the needs of what will be a rural populace, as we simultaneously plan and build for the city of our future. In anticipation of those needs we have incorporated the Soul City Foundation as the social planning arm of the project. That organization has, in turn, applied for and received a grant from the Department of Health, Education and Welfare for the establishment of an ambulatory health center—HealthCo, Inc. This organization is now operating a primary health care facility in two double-wide mobile units on the Soul City site. As part of a program to reach the rural residents of this region, HealthCo has instituted a Home Health Care Program to provide nursing care in the home on a regular basis.

Floyd B. McKissick Enterprises, Inc., the original developer of Soul City, has donated an 18th century plantation house, just recently named to the National Register of Historic Sites, to the Foundation. Known as the "Foundation House," it serves as a center for social life on the project. During the day it provides facilities for the local

Head Start program; at night and on weekends, local residents are offered classes in cultural and physical arts. On holidays, the Foundation House is the focal point for community festivities.

The Soul City Foundation has also just completed a year-long innovative educational program to encourage local junior high school students to achieve their full academic potential. Known as the Learning Lab, the program reached 130 economically and/or culturally disadvantaged children in the area with special small-group classes in math, reading, composition, drama, social studies, creative writing, media workshops, voice and diction in reading, dance, and arts and crafts, as well as group counseling and discussion sessions. The Learning Lab also developed a parent program to help build positive parent attitudes toward education in an area without an active parents' organization in connection with the school system. The Soul City Company has also offered the Warren County Board of Education a site in the new community's planned educational park to build a consolidated high school for the county.

In meeting the problems of the poor and uneducated residents of the local area, we are most interested in planning a community where people can be trained with marketable skills. The Foundation is now building, with partial funding from the Office of Economic Opportunity, the first industrial incubator facility in Soul City. When the structure is completed, the industry located there should provide fulltime, better employment for 300 people. In addition, the Foundation is now involved in a Manpower Program to identify the unemployed and underemployed persons in the labor force to help them locate jobs and job training both in Soul City and in the surrounding area.

To aid the local underprivileged businessman, we have the Warren Regional Planning Corporation (WRPC), a nonprofit organization funded by the Department of Commerce, Office of Minority Business Enterprise.

WRPC is composed of both a Business Development Organization (BDO) and a Construction Contractors Assistance Center (CCAC). These entities provide technical assistance to minority entrepreneurs and contractors in setting up business and securing contracts for construction in Soul City and the surrounding area.

As should be evident from the information presented so far, we at Soul City see economic development as the primary basis on which to build our social dreams into realities. Although new communities in general have been under fire recently for failure to meet either financial or social goals, Soul City has a good chance of success in both areas.

The Center for Urban and Regional Studies at the University of North Carolina has published a preliminary report on its research into the evaluation of established new communities by those who live there. Although new towns generally were found not to live up to residents' expectations, blacks formed one element who have been pleased with the improved living environments they found.

The assumption that new communities can start anew without racism seems to be legitimate. Soul City, as the boldest experiment in building a totally integrated, black-led, racism-free new community hopes to emulate previous successes on a much more extensive scale. We have been encouraged by very real accomplishments during the first year of our development plan, and invite any true adventurers to come join us in our efforts to see the Soul City dream through to complete reality.

5. Using Psychology in New Town Planning

STANLEY A. MURRELL

Any human community can be thought of as an interface between society and its resident-individuals. As the "middle" part of this set, the new town, through informed planning, has the potential to perhaps improve individual–society relationships. Any new town, however, will be continually buffeted by the realities of society, individuals, and the information base of its planning. To begin, a quick look at some of these realities seems to be in order.

New towns, whatever their size or location, are not isolated and independent islands but are component subparts of society. As such, society's problems limit the benefit new towns can be expected to provide, e.g., the nation's economic condition will affect prices and jobs in new towns, government scandals will affect new town resident's perceptions of their government officials, fuel and food shortages would be felt in new towns as well as old towns.

Another societal reality is persistent change. The population swings back and forth between more conservative and more liberal political attitudes. There are presently challenges to long-held values about work, inter-sex and inter-age relations, parenting, and family adaptiveness. Increases in pollution and traffic congestion; decreases in food and fuel will demand changes. Continuing social problems that have been barely touched by innumerable piecemeal restorative-rehabilitative programs will demand new methods of attack. The continuing conflictive relations among different racial and socioeconomic groups will increasingly threaten society's survival and will require change. Given this consistency of change, a new town cannot be a fixed island utopia—societal changes will require that the new town change.

The inevitability of and demand for change may eventually direct society, through government, toward the large-scale development of new towns. If new towns are seen as solutions to social problems, then psychosocial planning will rise in importance to the level of physical planning and economic considerations. In this event, the products of psychology will be scrutinized for their application value. Psychology will have to make some changes in order to provide usable information.

Using past history as a guide, I would predict that new towns would be "sold" to society as *the* "perfect solution" to all problems by both political figures and new town professionals. However, any expectation that new towns will be utopian is unrealistic.[1] A new town cannot be any "better" than the people who live in it, the planners who design it, or those who manage it. Utopian solutions assume a static relationship between individuals and environments whereas in reality the environment is constantly changing and individuals change in adapting to it. Since people and society change, even if an ideal new town could be designed for 1984, it would not be ideal in 1994. It is also a reality that new towns to date have been "new" primarily in the physical sense. New designs and construction do not by themselves make a utopia.

It is also to be expected that utopian claims for new

[1] Early indications from the North Carolina studies of new towns give ample evidence as to their imperfections.

towns will not go unchallenged. Such opponents may very well attack directly the psychosocial design, perhaps raising fears of Skinnerian "thought control" or a socialistic planning that requires rigid conformity by all.

Such charges are not completely unfounded. It is a reality that new towns require huge financial investments. Investors, whether they be private or public, will require accountability and, quite appropriately, control over the new town. Balancing control by investor with control by residents will be a continuing problem. Another reality is that the wide range of values, preferences, and behaviors of a resident population cannot be totally accommodated by a new town. As in any community, new towns will impose some constraints on individual choices.

It is in their psychosocial aspects that new towns are probably most vulnerable to their critics. This stems from the very nature of the social sciences and from the limited degree of applicability of research findings. For psychology, its data base consists largely of questionnaire responses and laboratory behavior; only a small proportion consists of systematic, objective observation of human behavior in natural settings. Its information is based largely on small groups, with only a small proportion of work on large organizations and with the work on total communities a rare exception (viz, Barker & Schoggen, 1973). It is only recently that the field has paid serious attention to the effect of the natural environment on behavior. Furthermore, the primary purpose of psychology as a science has been to understand, predict, and control separate psychological phenomena, not to apply its findings to real problems. Fortunately, however, there are areas of psychology that are at least related to psychosocial planning areas: the study of individual differences, the study of inter-group relations, studies from organizational psychology, recent research on the physical environment's effect on behavior, the social learning approaches to behavior, ecological psychology, and the study of individual–environment interactions.

AREAS FOR PSYCHOSOCIAL PLANNING

My primary experience for new town psychosocial planning comes from my work on the New Communities Family Mobility System (NewCom) that was developed by the Urban Studies Center at the University of Louisville. NewCom is a general model for the planning of new towns as responses to poverty. It is generally applicable for new towns located near the outer limits of medium-sized metropolitan cities with below-average unemployment. The designing of this model, which provides an integrated system of preoperational performance standards, required consideration not only of relocated poor families but also of the general habitability of all residents —in short, an environment was required that was psychosocially responsive to a wide range of individual differences. Parts of the model have been used or adapted in other new towns, for example Rural New Town, Inc., in Florida, and Woodlands outside Houston; and parts have been used in various community development projects. The detailed design and performance standards are available in the project report (Urban Studies Center, 1971) and I have discussed NewCom in the context of social interventions elsewhere (Murrell, 1973).

In the course of developing the psychosocial design for NewCom, we were confronted repeatedly with choices in critical areas. Some of these areas would appear to be basic to new town design in general and therefore appropriate for discussion here. Within each of these areas I will refer to selected psychological research to illustrate some of the kinds of information that would be relevant to the new town planner.

Power Distribution

Authority relations, lines of accountability, and decision-making structures are generally considered critical areas for organizations. For new towns, the psychosocial design must consider who has control and who is accountable for what, what the input channels into decision making should be, and the appropriate power balance between initial investors (private developers or government) and residents. The workability and the acceptance of such a balance, and more generally of the power distribution structure, will change over time. An acceptable distribution in the first three years of a new town may not hold for the tenth year. Thus, the psychosocial design must include a process for change in the power distribution that is both orderly and adaptive to changes in the resident-population and in society.

Some research from organizational psychology suggests that wide participation in decision making contributes to satisfaction and productivity (Likert, 1961). However, there is also evidence that this result depends on the size of the organization and the nature of the task (Porter & Lawler, 1965), and the work orientation of the population as well as the characteristics of the surrounding community (Hulin & Blood, 1968). Further, there is research that suggests that people with certain kinds of personality-behavioral characteristics will not have the resources or will be made anxious by strong pressure for participation in decision making (e.g., Lefcourt & Ladwig, 1965; Watson & Baumal, 1967). Therefore, it would appear that there are so many different variables involved that a new town planner could not determine in advance any one best power distribution structure that would be acceptable beyond a few years.

There is a general finding from behavior modification and social learning research that is also of relevance to power distribution: positive reinforcements from the environment are powerful determinants of behavior whereas punishment generally is not. This would suggest new town designs that provided positive reinforcement for desired behaviors, rather than punitive controls as are

now prevalent. (Criminal, antisocial, or destructive behaviors are now punished, but law-abiding, prosocial, or
protective-maintenance behaviors are not reinforced.)

A crucial point here is *who* decides what is desirable
behavior. If planners or managers decide on the behaviors
to be reinforced, then new towns can quite rightly be
criticized as being coercive. If the resident-population
decides on its behavioral objectives, such criticism is less
well founded. Studer (1972) has nicely described how basic learning principles can be used in environmental design but always within the context that the objective of
such designs is to realize the social goals of the population.
This suggests that there be an advance plan for the systematic measuring of the social goals of the population
repeatedly over time.

Size of Social/Physical Groupings

Here the question from the physical planner is: how
many dwelling units should there be in a neighborhood
(or cluster or village or whatever the grouping). Drawing
upon the work of ecological psychologists it would be
expected that in smaller size groupings, or "undermanned" groupings where there are more jobs to be done
per number of persons, residents will participate to a
greater degree, will feel more valued and more successful, will be evaluated less negatively by others, and will
feel a stronger sense of obligation than those in larger
"overmanned" settings (e.g., Barker & Gump, 1964;
Gump, 1972). Price (1974) interprets this research as sug-
gesting that undermanned settings have more potential
for developing psychological growth.

The data and methods of this research are having some
impact on psychology and in many ways they are the most
readily applicable to new towns that psychology has to
offer. This halo should not, however, beguile the new
town planner into using these findings indiscriminately.
While the obligation to participate may be a good experi-

ence for some people, others may feel a coercive, anxiety-producing pressure and intrusion. Undermanned settings should be considered as providing growth experiences for *some* people, not as an *absolute* good to be applied to all residents. Thus, the new town planner will need to think in terms of the advantages of smaller as opposed to larger groupings. The smaller the grouping the fewer services and facilities it can support, and therefore choices for individuals are more limited.

Population Mix

Here the question boils down to the spatial arrangement of differently priced dwelling units. The trade-off is between social comfort on the one hand and socioeconomic integration (or the avoidance of intergroup conflicts between social classes) on the other.

There is considerable evidence that social comfort is enhanced by similarities in race, religion, ethnicity, occupations, values, and age (e.g., Broxton, 1962; Festinger, 1950; Gans, 1970; Newcomb, 1956, 1958). There is also evidence that social relations among groups are improved under democratic, cooperative, equal status situations (e.g., Deutsch & Collins, 1958; Irish, 1952; Wilner, Wakely, & Cook, 1952).

On the basis of this kind of research, in the NewCom model the face-to-face groupings (clusters) were designed to be homogeneous with respect to housing price and types (suitable to the same age families). However, with neighborhoods (common schools) and villages (common governance systems) there would be a wide range of cost and housing type. While there was similarity within clusters, there was variation among them.

Matching Person and Environment

In a general sense, the psychosocial purpose of new towns could be defined as optimizing the *match* between what individuals need and prefer in terms of services and opportunities and what the community provides and positively reinforces. While conceptually this goal seems to make sense, there are problems involving the lack of uniformity of individual behavior across different environments.

A number of studies on individual–environment interactions (e.g., Endler & Hunt, 1966, 1968, 1969; Moos, 1968, 1969; Prescott, 1973; Raush, Dittman, & Taylor, 1959; Raush, Farbman, & Llewellyn, 1960; Schuster, 1973) have shown rather consistent findings: the same individual behaves differently in different situations; within the same situation different people behave differently, i.e., the same situation has different meanings for different individuals. Individual and situational characteristics *interact* so that behavior is determined by a mixture of both. The strength of individual characteristics relative to the strength of situational characteristics in determining behavior is not set in any fixed ratio but varies with such characteristics as age, sex, I.Q., and psychiatric status and is different for different behaviors (e.g., anxiousness being more situationally influenced than hostility). This is not to say that there are no individual trans-situational consistencies; there are, and there are trans-individual consistencies for situations. But these consistencies predict only a portion of the behavior; the interaction effect accounts for a significant (and often a relatively larger) proportion of the behavior.

For psychology this means that the precise prediction of specific behaviors for a particular individual in all situations is not possible. Only rather gross (and often trivial) behavior patterns highly common to a particular situation (e.g., sitting and driving behavior on an expressway) can be predicted with great confidence. Thus there is support for science fiction writer Isaac Asimov's "prediction" (in his *Foundation* trilogy) of a science of "psychohistory" that can accurately predict events and directions of societies over hundreds of years, but is yet unable to predict the behaviors of individuals.

This unpredictability of individual behavior means that no single new town can possibly provide utopian matches for all individuals since all varieties of their behaviors could not be known or accommodated. The planner can anticipate only gross behavior patterns. Moreover, the behavior patterns of persons in their "old" community would probably not continue to be the same in the changed environment of a new town. Thus, even if the old behavior characteristics of residents could be known precisely in advance, their predictive value for the new town would be low.

Any one new town design, then, will have multiple effects as it interacts with widely differing individual characteristics and these effects cannot be adequately anticipated. From the standpoint of improving individual–society relations in general, a *series* of new towns should be planned with each having clearly different psychosocial priorities. This would enlarge the choices for individuals and perhaps improve the quality of individual–new town matches.

NEW TOWNS AS EXPERIMENTING COMMUNITIES

It seems to me to be counter-productive to think of new towns as utopian final solutions. Their function should be seen as a *means* toward improvement of individual–society relationships rather than an idealistic *end* state. As large-scale, on-going social experiments, they can increasingly provide information on the attainment of social goals by different new town designs for different populations. Of course this would require that the regular systematic collection of social goal information be planned for in the design. It would also require that each new town be designed to differ from other new towns. In a step-wise manner, such information could then be used for further new town planning. If a cycle could be established wherein the psychosocial information is collected from extant different new towns, and then carried through and used in planning future new towns, which in turn would yield information for even further new towns, it would be of great value to the science of new town design, the science of psychology, and to individual–society relations in general. We can hope to improve the process without expecting a permanently ideal product.

REFERENCES

Barker, R. G. & Gump, P. V. *Big school, small school.* Stanford, Calif.: Stanford University Press, 1964.

Barker, R. G. & Schoggen, P. *Qualities of community life.* San Francisco: Jossey-Bass, 1973.

Broxton, J. A method of predicting roommate compatibility for college freshmen. *Journal of the National Association of Women Deans and Counselors,* 1962, *21,* 602–605.

Deutsch, M. & Collins, M. The effect of public policy in housing projects upon interracial attitudes. In E. Maccoby, T. M. Newcomb & E. L. Hartley (Eds.), *Readings in social psychology.* New York: Holt, 1958.

Endler, N. & Hunt, J. McV. Sources of behavioral variance as measured by the S-R Inventory of Anxiousness. *Psychological Bulletin,* 1966, *65,* 336–346.

Endler, N. & Hunt, J. McV. S-R Inventories of hostility and comparisons of the proportions of variance from persons, responses, and situations for hostility and anxiousness. *Journal of Personality and Social Psychology,* 1968, *9,* 309–315.

Endler, N. & Hunt, J. McV. Generalizability of contributions from sources of variance in the S-R Inventories of Anxiousness. *Journal of Personality,* 1969, *37,* 1–24.

Festinger, L. Laboratory experiments: The role of group belongingness. In J. G. Miller (Ed.), *Experiments in social process.* New York: McGraw-Hill, 1950.

Gans, H. J. Planning and social life: friendship and neighbor relations in suburban communities. In H. M. Pro-
shausky, W. H. Ittelson, & L. G. Rivlin (Eds.),
Environmental psychology. New York: Holt, Rinehart, 1970. Pp. 501–509.

Gump, P. Linkages between the "ecological environment" and behavior and experience of persons. In W.
M. Smith (Ed.), *Behavior design, and policy aspects of
human habitats.* Green Bay: University of Wisconsin
at Green Bay, 1972.

Hulin, C. & Blood, M. Job enlargement, individual differences, and worker responses. *Psychological Bulletin,*
1968, *69,* 41–55.

Irish, D. P. Reactions of caucasian residents to Japanese-
American neighbors. *Journal of Social Issues,* 1952,
8, 10–17.

Lefcourt, H. & Ladwig, G. The effect of reference group
upon Negroes task persistence in a biracial competitive game. *Journal of Personality and Social Psychology,* 1965, 1, 668–670.

Likert, R. *New patterns of management.* New York:
McGraw-Hill, 1961.

Moos, R. H. Situational analysis of a therapeutic community milieu. *Journal of Abnormal Psychology,* 1968,
73, 49–61.

Moos, R. H. Sources of variance in responses to question-
naires and in behavior. *Journal of Abnormal Psychology,* 1969, *74,* 405–412.

Murrell, S. *Community psychology and social systems.*
New York: Behavioral Publications, 1973.

Newcomb, T. M. The prediction of interpersonal attraction. *American Psychologist,* 1956, *11,* 575–586.

Newcomb, T. M. The cognition of persons as cognizers. In
R. Tagiuri & L. Petrullo (Eds.), *Person perception and
interpersonal behavior.* Stanford, Calif.: Stanford
University Press, 1958.

Price, R. H. Etiology, the social environment, and the
prevention of psychological dysfunction. In P. Lugel

& R. H. Moos (Eds.), *Health and the social environment.* Lexington, Mass.: D. C. Heath, 1974.

Porter, L. W. & Lawler, E. E., III. Properties of organizational structure in relation to job attitudes and job behavior. *Psychological Bulletin,* 1965, *64,* 23–51.

Prescott, E. Assessment of child-rearing environments: an ecological approach. *Part 2 of Final Report for Children's Bureau, Office of Child Development, U.S. Department of Health, Education and Welfare # R-219(C6).* Pasadena: Pacific Oaks College, 1973.

Raush, H., Dittman, A., & Taylor, T. Person, setting, and change in social interaction. *Human Relations,* 1959, *12,* 361–378.

Raush, H. L., Farbman, I., & Llewellyn, L. G. Person, setting and change in social interaction: II. A normal control study. *Human Relations,* 1960, *13,* 305–332.

Schuster, S. An ecological analysis of preschool children's social behaviors. Unpublished doctoral dissertation, Louisville: University of Louisville, 1973.

Studer, R. G. Behavior contingent design of non-environment systems. In W. M. Smith (Ed.), *Behavior, design, and policy aspects of human habitats.* Green Bay: University of Wisconsin at Green Bay, 1972.

Urban Studies Center, University of Louisville. *The new communities family mobility system.* Louisville, Ky.: University of Louisville Urban Studies Center, 1971.

Watson, D., & Baumal, E. Effects of locus of control and expectation of future control upon present performance. *Journal of Personality and Social Psychology,* 1967, *6,* 212–215.

Wilner, D. M., Wakely, R. P. & Cook, S. W. Residential proximity and intergroup relations in public housing projects. *Journal of Social Issues,* 1952, *8,* 45–69.

Section II

THE NEW TOWN AS A LABORATORY OF HUMAN RELATIONS: THE CASE OF COLUMBIA, MARYLAND

6. *Introduction*

Section II takes up different facets of Columbia's social, psychological, and institutional status. Written seven or eight years after Columbia's inception, the papers represent varied perspectives: residents, social scientists, agency directors, and developer-planners. While they in no way represent a systematic appraisal, they are intended to provide a variety of experiential handles which the reader can use in order to grasp the nature of Columbia as a venture in comprehensive community planning and design.

It is, of course, difficult to grasp the essence of any community, even those with distinctive characters that have been formed over many years. In the case of Columbia the task is more difficult because its ultimate essence has yet to emerge. As these words are being written the community has about 38,000 residents; it is intended to grow to 110,000 by the early to mid-1980's. It is a rapidly growing settlement composed largely of young middle-class families with preschool and school age children, though it does have a substantial number of single persons and a growing proportion of elderly people. It is a racially open community and about 15 to 20 percent of the population is black. There are some relatively low-income families (though few at the poverty level), most of whom live in subsidized, nonprofit rental town houses and apartment units scattered through Columbia's several villages. The population tends to be politically liberal, college educated, and involved in community affairs. Less than one-third of Columbia's wage earners work in the city, despite the fact that the community includes large industrial parks and a growing number of office buildings.

Elsewhere (Klein, 1968) I have suggested that the essential meta-functions of any community are three-fold: (1) to provide for its inhabitants' physical and psychological safety and security; (2) to provide resources needed to cope with the varied problems of living throughout the life cycle; and (3) to afford a basis for each inhabitant's social significance. Though none of the following articles addresses itself directly to the above three community functions, each contributes in some way to an understanding of how well Columbia is doing with respect to them. The articles are intended to share with the reader the dynamics of how the community has been grappling, successfully and unsuccessfully, with the various challenges involved.

In his contribution James W. Rouse, the developer of Columbia, presents the conceptual base for that community and the steps taken to move from concept to reality. He describes how a consultant work group drawn largely from the behavioral sciences contributed to the process of designing a community that would provide "a sense of place at each level." Rouse makes a persuasive case for building thoughtfully planned new towns as better alternatives to suburban sprawl and urban clutter.

The next paper (by Peter Wastie, a member of the Columbia development team, and myself) discusses the process of "institutional development" whereby the social systems and institutions of the new town were devised and set into place. Institutional development is not the same as Organization Development (OD), which has come to mean the rational-technical means whereby techniques from the applied behavioral sciences are used to bring about change within existing organizations. Institutional development refers to the design and installation of new organizational means for meeting the various needs and wants of a community's population. For the present, institutional development remains an artistic process that has been neither conceptualized nor researched. This paper is presented as a case study of the institutional development process in one new town, from which the reader is invited to draw his or her own generalizations.

The next three papers in Section II take up in more detail specific instances of institutional development which occurred in Columbia as the result of citizen initiative as needs for human service institutions were identified. The first, written by Allan Feinstein at a time when he was Executive Director of Grassroots, a crisis counseling service, traces the development of that agency from the perspective of a community psychologist interested in conceptualizing the process of change within a complicated social system. The second paper, written by Lynn and Paul Shoffeit, a husband-wife team of community psychologists, describes the development of the Family Life Center, an innovative counseling, educational, and information center for strengthening family life. The third traces the development and functions of the Women's Center, which was spawned by the Columbia Cooperative Ministry (an association of Protestant ministers) and based originally at the Interfaith Center (one of Columbia's unique institutions). Written by its initiator Louise Eberhardt, the paper focuses on how the Center helps both married and single women engage in self-discovery; redefine their familial roles; and bridge gaps between their familial, community, and occupational lives.

Eberhardt's paper serves as a bridge to the final portion of Section II, which turns to a consideration of specific subgroups whose special needs pose challenges to all those concerned about the design and development of well-functioning communities. In addition to women in modern society, the list of such special groups might include singles of both sexes, one-parent families, blacks and other ethnic minorities, poor people, senior citizens, and teenagers. Singled out for special attention in this issue are blacks and teenagers.

Black Involvement in a New Community is written by someone who has both lived and worked in Columbia for some time. Jean Warrick Toomer, an early resident of the city, was for several years an employee of the Columbia Association as Director of Community Services and later Director of Volunteer Services. Her contribution, written from the viewpoint of a black citizen and professional person, acknowledges Columbia's achievements as a well-designed physical social environment. It goes on to document ways in which the community—open as it is to ethnic minorities—falls short of being the fully integrated, nonracist city dreamed about by McKissick in his contribution to this issue.

Finally, Roger Karsk, President of the Community Research and Action Laboratory (CoRAL II) in Columbia, and I report on "Teenagers in Columbia" based, in part, on detailed logs of their activities maintained by a group of teenagers during an entire year. The report represents one of the few in-depth studies undertaken of any aspect of Columbia's development since its inception. The fact that little systematic research of a psychological nature has been undertaken in the community may come as a surprise, given the involvement of social scientists and human services experts in its original planning. There are at least three reasons why so little research has been carried out: (1) the developer has been understandably reluctant to expose residents to a barrage of inquiries for fear of engendering resentment about living in a fishbowl, thereby jeopardizing residential sales; (2) the community is moving through a period of a rapid growth, from a small hamlet to a middle-sized town in the course of only a few years, thereby making it difficult to conduct anything but

prospective longitudinal studies of shifts in certain phenomena over time; and (3) there has been curious reluctance on the part of federal agencies to invest research
funds even in studies proposed by nonprofit social science
groups wishing to study Columbia. Such reluctance appears to have stemmed from a disinclination either to
subsidize a private developer, even indirectly, or to encourage the channeling of money and energies away from
inner-city problems by taking seriously the experimental
potentials of the new town movement. A refreshing exception was the willingness of National Institute of Mental
Health's Center for Metropolitan Studies to provide a
grant in support of the youth study reported herein.

If Columbia is any indication, there is something about
a new town which spawns a ferment of ideas and social
innovations. Everyone is new together; in its early stages
the community is a virtual blank slate on which anyone
can attempt to trace institutional designs without running
afoul of vested interests and conflicting jurisdictions. The
ferment in Columbia was stimulated by the existence of
a framework established by the developer for encouraging citizen initiative. For example, Antioch College students helped launch Grassroots as a counterculture
counseling center, and Antioch was encouraged to establish its Columbia center in the hope that it might provide
a kind of social yeast for the community. As already noted,
the Interfaith Center furnished the impetus, staff support,
funding, and physical shelter for the Women's Center.
The Family Life Center, in turn, was supported wholeheartedly by the developer because it brought into being
many aspects of a Family Life Institute concept proposed
by the initial work group of social scientists.

In addition to being potential spawning grounds for
new ideas, new towns also appear to be prone to the
malaise of unrealistic expectations. The problem appears
both among those participating in the community's development and those choosing subsequently to establish enterprises in the new "Shangri-la." Among those who have

tended to move prematurely to the new city (when, in fact, its population barely exceeded that of a small village) have been proprietors of human service institutions, cultural agencies, and business enterprises. The result has been a string of failures involving such varied enterprises as art and music programs, schools of theater and dance, institutions of higher education, grocery stores, and shops of various kinds. Among the casualties was the first version of the Community Research and Action Laboratory with which I was associated.

I can testify from personal experience that the vision of a fully planned garden city excites the imagination and also tends to dull the critical judgment which might otherwise function. The institutions described in Section II so far have survived the economic reaper. In no instances, however, have they avoided continuing and often desperate financial struggles engendered, at least in part, by the lack in a new community of an adequate charitable or other financial base on which to erect certain badly needed social institutions.

REFERENCE

Klein, D. C. *Community dynamics and mental health.* New York: John Wiley & Sons, 1968.

7. Building a Sense of Place

JAMES W. ROUSE

Looking at the random, reckless sprawl that reaches out from our cities, it seemed reasonable to believe in 1962 as, indeed, it does today that the artifacts of urban growth—dwellings, schools, clinics, recreation facilities, shops, services and employment centers—could be brought together in a more rational way than the suburban sprawl and commercial clutter which marks the expansion of our cities. Shouldn't it be possible to deal with the land in a more sensitive way—preserving streams, valleys, hillsides, and flood plains and concentrating development where it best ought to occur? Couldn't the living and working areas that man builds enoble the land rather than desecrate it? Shouldn't it be possible to build communities in which school, church, health, and recreation institutions would relate to each other and the people they served in a more supportive way? Couldn't there be a richer sense of community among people if the physical place and the community institutions were all seen as opportunities to support and enable the growth of people?

These are the kinds of questions we asked over and over again in our company and which led us to undertake the task of building a city. We believed that it would be economically feasible and socially important to build a new community which would demonstrate that there is, in fact, a better way for a city to grow than through sprawl and clutter.

Our first step in planning Columbia (after we assembled the land) was to bring together a work group of people from a variety of disciplines to share ideas on the crucial issues of urban life; to explore in an interdisciplinary way the optimums in education, health, religion, recreation, employment, housing, etc.; to examine successes and failures in urban and suburban communities; to learn more about how the planning and development of community could contribute to the life and growth of the human individual and the family. This work group consisted of people drawn largely from the behavioral sciences who had worked in health, education, employment, communication; who had worked with and studied urban life and its consequences.

We met every two weeks, and each meeting was for at least two days and a night for a period of about four months. Our planning and development staff participated fully in the meetings.

At the same time we were recording in detail the physical conditions of the land itself and reporting them in such a way that the land could speak to us about where and how physical development should occur and where it should be protected.

We were not attempting to design a contemporary utopia but simply to gain a better perspective on urban life. We wanted to see what made it good and bad and how we might make it better through physical planning and development. We did not ask the work group for conclusions or even for recommendations or reports. We wanted "shafts of light" to guide us just as the data derived from the land itself would point directions for the physical response to the land. We wanted deeper understanding of the issues and the possibilities involved in urban growth. We said, "Let's look at the optimums—

don't worry about feasibility. Feasibility will compromise us soon enough. Let's see what might best be, in order that we can have a star to navigate towards."

The work group process was extremely helpful. It made us wiser; equipped us better to plan and to develop a new community. It did not produce any brilliant new concepts or sociological breakthroughs nor was it intended to. It simply permitted us to do a much better job of craftsmanship in bringing the elements of a city together so that they might work to make life better for the people who lived there. The plan that evolved was focused on producing a sense of community at various levels from the cul-de-sac or block to the neighborhood, to the village and to the city as a whole.

We believed it was important to produce a sense of place at each level of community to which a person felt a sense of belonging and in which it might be easy to meet and know his neighbors. (It is this absence of central places and physical scale in typical metropolitan sprawl that bleeds away the opportunity for community.) A gang mail box at the heart of a cul-de-sac would induce meetings as in a commercial water well. At the heart of the neighborhood would be an elementary school, nursery school, park, playground, swimming pool, and meeting room. A path system would lead easily to the neighborhood center.

At the heart of a village would be a high school and middle school, churches, library, community rooms, recreation center, supermarket, bank, restaurant, and small stores. The village would be a small town of about 12,000 people. Like the neighborhoods, it would be physically identifiable separated by other villages by the open space system. The village center would result in un-self-conscious, unplanned, unregimented meetings among children, parents, teachers, merchants, ministers while conducting their daily lives. Provision was made for the election of a village board to be a voice for the community in dealing with the developer, the county, and with other communities. The village board would designate committees to deal with village circumstances: recreation, transportation, early childhood training, and special needs as they arose. Schools would serve as centers of activity for the neighborhoods and the village beyond regular school hours.

At the center of the eight villages there would be a downtown with services for the entire city: department stores, shops, restaurants, banks, hotels, office buildings, theatres, concert halls, colleges, hospital, etc. The downtown area would not only serve the entire city but would exert a polarizing force in causing the people of the villages to feel a larger community in the city as a whole. This large sense of community would be amplified by the existence of a city-wide organization (Columbia Association) to own and operate the lakes, parks, open spaces, and recreation facilities; to run public transportation; to provide early childhood training and day care; to provide programs of recreation, education, and entertainment; to respond to community needs and yearnings.

In early 1976 these beginning concepts of Columbia have been carefully carried forward. There are 40,000 people living in six villages with four completed village centers. Neighborhoods and villages are both separated and connected by an open space system of nearly 2,000 acres. There are eleven elementary schools, three middle schools, and two high schools; colleges and graduate programs, and a hospital. Villages are connected to downtown by a bus system, and downtown has a strong beginning with two department stores, shops, hotel, cinema, office buildings, restaurants, and other services.

Columbia is, in fact, a small city within an array of commercial and public facilities that was never found in random suburban development. It is culturally and economically diverse and racially open.

The planning and development on city-scale has had important impact on the institutions of city. It has held out new possibilities for existing institutions and released creative energy for change in response to the new opportunities.

Thus, in a conservative, largely rural county, the school board has delivered a public school system widely considered to be one of the most advanced in America with open classrooms, team teaching, and emphasis on the development of the individual child. The success of this open school system has, in turn, affected and is rapidly transforming the school system in the balance of the county.

Institutions of the three major faiths responded to the opportunity to think and plan on city-scale by creating a Religious Facilities Corporation which owns the church buildings at the heart of the villages. The integrity of the faith and theology of the individual denominations is preserved in a setting in which priests, nuns, rabbis, and ministers share office space and facilities and work together in joint programs to serve their congregations and the community. Together they formed a nonprofit housing corporation that has built subsidized housing for people of moderate income in the city.

The Johns Hopkins Medical Institutions saw the opportunity to bring preventive health care, group medical practice, and hospital services to an entire community through a prepaid comprehensive health care system. This has resulted in the Columbia Medical Plan which now delivers full health care including hospital, catastrophe coverage, and psychiatric counseling to almost 40% of the population on a monthly prepaid basis.

Most important is Columbia's racial openness when compared with the segregation in housing that marks the suburbs surrounding virtually all American cities. Lying in a suburban county that is overwhelmingly white, between two cities that are overwhelmingly black, is a racially open city in which blacks feel full proprietorship with whites in their communities. In the resale of housing in the secondary market, houses move from black to white as readily as white to black. This is crucial to a truly open community.

Thoughtful observers of life in Columbia have noted the prevailing ethos of the community in the attitude people hold towards their city, their institutions, and their future. Whereas the malaise of the old city and its suburbs is often identified as emerging from a sense of helplessness and hopelessness about the conditions that surround them, it is fair to say that in Columbia there is a prevailing mood among people that they can do something about what molests life or causes it not to work well; that they can exert effective initiative to bring about change.

This initiative is frequently taken to build new institutions to meet new needs. Grassroots, the Family Life Center, the Women's Center are examples of that initiative. Columbia Gardeners was organized to provide garden plot opportunities for apartment dwellers, and there were more than 1,000 participants last year. The women of Oakland Mills brought into being the Oakland Mills Post Office, the only volunteer post office in America. Schools for theater, ballet, and music along with art galleries, political clubs, and dozens of special interest groups thrive in the city. There are 106 voluntary organizations listed in the Columbia telephone directory. The directory itself represents the unique initiative of a Columbia woman who prints profitably, a directory that lists not only name, street, and telephone number but, also, the first name of the unlisted spouse, the neighborhood, and the village of each resident. Some organizations that once served a useful purpose, like Friendship Exchange, have faded away, perhaps because the purpose or leadership faded. The dissolution of community efforts cannot be regarded as failure, but as a part of vitality in dynamic community. An environment that encourages the effort to try, to initiate, to create will bring forth a wide range of results from sparkling new institutions and services to short-lived efforts that "couldn't make it."

It is important to see Columbia in relationship to its objective; to demonstrate that there is a better alternative to suburban sprawl and clutter in accommodating the growth of America's metropolitan centers, and that alternative is the thoughtfully planned new community. Our cities will continue to grow. Even with zero population growth, we will add more than 25,000 new households each week for the next 15 years. These new households will be formed by men and women already born in the period following World War II. In the years ahead we will have more women of childbearing age than we have ever known in the history of our country. With fewer children per mother, we will still have the largest number of new babies in our history. The well planned new community produces a quality of life and community that is impossible through random, scattered subdivision development. The important contribution of the new community to the growth and life of the individual and the family is overlooked when Columbia is judged by the gap between what it is and what might be. It was never intended to be the perfect city nor will it ever be. It was intended to be a "better city"—much better than the sprawl and clutter that would have unfolded on its land through the normal process of growth. There are lessons to be learned from its experience which are of enormous importance to America. It is time to recognize the critical importance of new communities in the growth of our cities, time to recognize the meaning that rational community has for the growth of individuals and families. The continuance of sprawl and clutter is reckless and extravagant in the use of money, land, and human lives. We know better, and we should do better.

8. An Approach to Institutional Development

PETER WASTIE
DONALD C. KLEIN

In an abbreviated way, this paper attempts to trace the process of institutional development in the new town of Columbia, Maryland, and suggests a few generalizations about the process that may be applicable to other localities. In the Columbia context, institutional development is taken to mean those aspects of planning and development which deal with the social systems and institutions of the new town.

Institutional development in Columbia, as in any new town, is a result of *scale*. By the time the work group of social scientists and specialists from various fields was convened in 1963 to begin the process of Columbia's institutional development, 14,000 acres had already been purchased and the commitment had been made to build a total city of 110,000 people. By working at such a scale, the scope of the project and the economics involved would be enough to allow changes in health, education, and other human service systems that would not be affordable in smaller scale undertakings.

The work group essentially was asked to carry out a brainstorming operation based on its members' expertise and dreams of what an optimal community might be like.

They were not to be concerned with such economic considerations as land sales, development costs, and the like. The economics, though complicated enough, seemed relatively straightforward to the developer. It was felt that residential land sales, industrial land sales, and commercial development (which is where the dollars come from) were matters that could be handled successfully based on the company's previous experiences, which were extensive though on a much smaller scale than was contemplated in Columbia.

The innovations sought for Columbia dealt with the development of social institutions. There was little new or startling about other aspects of the city, including both its economics and its architecture. Unlike its counterpart in Reston, Virginia, Columbia did not set out to make striking architectural statements. Its first housing consisted of a conservative set of detached colonial style homes intended to indicate that the new town would not constitute a shocking departure from existing residential areas in the County. The company had already announced that Columbia would be completely open racially, and it was believed that open housing (a fairly radical departure from existing norms of the area in 1963) might hurt the sale of homes unless the homes themselves did not deviate markedly in appearance from the existing housing market of Howard County.

MANAGEMENT OF INSTITUTIONAL DEVELOPMENT

An enormous amount of money was spent on institutional development, not only in planning and staff time, but also for consultants and work on such matters as proposals to the Ford Foundation to help the County's Board of Education become fully involved in planning educational improvements that would benefit both Columbia and the entire County. At any given time there were four to six senior members of the Rouse Company staff, representing about one-fourth of senior management, who in the early presettlement days were involved on a daily basis with some part of the social-institutional process. As Columbia began to take shape and building was underway, a Department of Institutional Development was created. Later mated with another department having to do with institutional relations, the department was concerned with strengthening relationships and providing support to agencies beginning to develop in Columbia as well as existing institutions in the surrounding region. In addition to the designated department, several senior management people remained deeply involved so that during the first five years (until about 1969) institutional development was carried on by anywhere from six to ten people. It is not surprising, therefore, that institutional development remains the single most dynamic quality of the community. When people talk about the distinctive characteristics of Columbia, they are most apt to focus on the medical plan, the nature of the schools, village centers and village government, the Columbia Association, and other social characteristics, rather than the architecture or technology of the city.

EDUCATIONAL DEVELOPMENT

In order to set the institutional development process in motion, certain critical decisions were made early in the presettlement phase. Perhaps most important was the decision to base the city's development on the neighborhood, at the hub of which would be an elementary school. This notion was totally dependent on the county's readiness to build small elementary schools on a neighborhood level. In order to implement the idea it was essential to develop close working relationships with the school system where the neighborhood school concept was not being used. The county had for some time been creating a system of regional schools, depending on bussing to collect students from rural sections and deposit them in central, easily accessible locations.

Once school officials agreed to the neighborhood school concept, it was essential to move to related components such as the location of middle and senior high schools. Within the long, involved process of work on size and location of school facilities, it also became possible to consider educational innovations that had worked well elsewhere, such as open space schools and team teaching. The work group had already made it clear that both physical and programmatic elements were basic to the design of up-to-date educational facilities. The shift of the County to open plan schools, team teaching, and the like expressed an educational approach that seemed consistent with sound educational practice as well as with the values and aspirations of the developer and of the people who might be attracted to a socially innovative new town. Economic considerations were essential as they generally are in all aspects of institutional development. From a practical economic standpoint, good schools are necessary to draw populations of families willing and able to invest in both housing and schooling for themselves and their offspring. It was assumed that such people would not move to a county that some had rated as having the next to the worst school system in Maryland.

Obviously it would have been both presumptuous and impractical for the developers to have recommended alterations based on their limited experience of what schools should be. Instead, school officials were helped to secure grants that were used to call in consultants with acknowledged expertise in education. Consultants from the Educational Facilities Lab were brought in to evaluate the entire system and make recommendations regarding how it might use Columbia's emergence as a means for making improvements throughout. In the end, possibly the most major innovation stimulated by Columbia was the overhauling of an entire county school system.

Work with the schools demonstrated the viability of the concept that major changes in social-institutional arrangements are facilitated if development proceeds at a sufficiently large scale. Here was a new residential development that came into a county and fostered change in an existing system, thus affecting education for people in the farther reaches of a county who otherwise were far removed from the new town itself.

DEVELOPMENT IN HEALTH CARE

Another important defining decision concerned health care. To its developer, Columbia represented a clean slate on which could be drawn a comprehensive health care system. Early in the presettlement period discussions were initiated with the Dean of the Johns Hopkins Medical School to determine how best to use the size of the projected population to develop better medical care than could be provided on a piecemeal basis. As it turned out, the Connecticut General Life Insurance Company, the Rouse Company's financial partner in Columbia and a large medical insurance carrier, became important to the prepaid medical plan that was hammered out. Essential to the institutional development process in this instance were three large resourceful elements: (1) a leading medical school faculty and facilities; (2) a major insurance carrier capable of underwriting a program that would, of necessity, operate at a loss for some time; and (3) a real estate developer with 14,000 acres to play with and a relatively captive population numbering 110,000 in the end. These resources were brought to bear on a virtual health vacuum. The County did not have a hospital of any kind, with an insufficient number of private practitioners to care for the projected population, a health department offering limited direct services, and an infinitesimal school health program. The entire medical system of the County was hardly adequate for its semi-rural nature by modern standards; it certainly would not meet the needs of an entire city.

When the prepaid medical program was initiated, it was expected that between 70 and 80 percent of Columbia's residents would participate so that only a very small number of private practitioners would be required. Initially, therefore, the institutional development group discouraged physicians from opening private practices in Columbia, both to enable the medical plan to develop the membership needed for a viable economic base and to alert the practitioner to possible hardships in competing with the plan.

To date the medical plan has not met the original expectations; only 35 to 40 percent of Columbia's residents belong. The care is excellent but the plan is prohibitively expensive for lower income people and too costly to attract the percentage of members that had been projected. There was no provision for dealing with those residents who could not afford membership. At present there is no real solution to that problem so that people who cannot afford $65 or $70 a month in medical premiums are excluded from the outstanding health care.

On the positive side, a most impressive characteristic of the Columbia medical plan is the psychiatric care provided at very low cost to plan members. There is an unusually high rate of use of psychiatric services (by comparison with other areas of the country having medical plans which provide psychiatric services), which suggests that some of the stigma from seeking mental health care has been eliminated. If so, several factors probably play a part. First, the social values of the population, reflected by the fact that the majority voted for McGovern in 1972, would characterize comparatively liberal people who are apt to attach positive values to seeking psychiatric assistance for relatively minor disorders. Second, and closely related, is the fact that a large percentage of resi-

64 THE NEW TOWN AS A LABORATORY

64 THE NEW TOWN AS A LABORATORY

dents are college graduates with many holding advanced degrees that would imply their willingness to enlist the aid of a mental health professional. Third, some positive leadership may have occurred since some early users were well-known people associated with the Rouse Company itself so that it became almost a prestigious matter to be involved personally with the mental health facility.

DEVELOPMENT OF RELIGIOUS FACILITIES

A third major area of institutional development culminated in the Interfaith Center, which provides a jointly owned facility for use by the various religious denominations. It made little economic or social sense to the developer to have 20 churches on 20 corners all scratching to pay off mortgages when it was possible, again beginning with a clean state and operating at a large enough scale, to join together in one building. The result would be less cost to each denomination and the benefits of being able to use more extensive, varied facilities within a single center. Implementation of the interfaith concept required a great deal of time and effort in order to persuade major denominations of the desirability and feasibility of the plan. Institutional development team members, supplemented by senior company officials as needed, visited local and regional representatives of major denominations, including, for example, the Roman Catholic and Episcopal archdioceses. In fact, the success of the concept was assured only when the Roman Catholic church, the single largest denomination, decided to take part. Since then the interfaith system, including a cooperative Protestant ministry, has been emerging, although sometimes with hesitation and difficulty.

An important consideration leading to the interfaith effort involved land planning and the economics of land use. It made sense from the developer's viewpoint to know ahead of time where all the churches were going to be, rather than having all denominations out in the marketplace trying to buy up land and possibly in the end making it necessary for the developer to subsidize their land purchases. From the outset, it was possible to lay out six sites for interfaith centers located in village centers so as to correspond with projected concentration of residents. This pattern also has the effect of not fostering homogeneous clusters of parishioners living close together because of proximity to separate parishes. The original concept was for each village to have its own interfaith facility. This model may well need to be revised. The first interfaith center is being used by residents from two adjacent villages, the second of which may never require a facility of its own. Some church groups also have found it convenient and economical to make use of general community center space rented from the Columbia Association, which uses the space during the week for other community purposes.

MULTIPLE USE FACILITIES

The interfaith center is an example of one kind of multiple use facility, the creation of which has figured prominently in the thinking of many new town social planners. The creation of shared multi-use structures was very appealing to Columbia's institutional development team for many reasons, both practical and idealistic. In practice, however, not all of the efforts have been as successful as the cooperative venture of church groups. For example, it was originally thought that the neighborhood school might become a 24 hour resource for the neighborhood —for meetings, recreation, church use, even family support and counseling services. Despite the enthusiasm of the development team, this did not happen as school administrators were not prepared to have their schools become multi-use community places. Their concerns were by no means theoretical; rather, they got down to such matters as: Who pays for gas and electricity? Who will control the use and preservation of the facility? What about additional insurance and custodial costs? What limitations, if any, can be placed on the use of ball fields and other areas by groups not associated with the schools? Because such questions could not be resolved to everyone's satisfaction, neighborhood schools in Columbia have not been put to the extensive multiple use originally contemplated.

Columbia's experience, by and large, if typical of our society, indicates that groups tend to seek their own territory, which they can control for their own use and make available on their own terms to outsiders. Each time the development team has created a structure for people to share it has worked only with great difficulty and sometimes less efficiently than had been expected. The multiuse theory is highly attractive, both financially and socially. Nonetheless, it has not fully lived up to the expectations of the development team. Far from being abandoned, however, it is being used in a delimited way in the design of a community theater for the newest village, which, because of the addition of a storage facility designed by the church groups, can also serve as a major facility for Sunday church services.

THE COLUMBIA ASSOCIATION

Possibly the most significant piece of institutional development in Columbia was the creation of the Columbia Association, a dominant force in almost all aspects of the community's life. It is often easy for social planners to overlook the fact that in most new communities institutional development will be needed in the area of government, politics, decision making, and the control of the community at least through its development period or until it is ready to become a legal municipality. The Columbia Association was established to provide such quasi-governmental functions in areas not already provided by county government. The Association is viable because it has an unusually strong economic base (compared to most homeowners associations and other such membership groups) because it was set up to parallel the County tax assessment formula. Seventy-five cents per one hundred dollars of assessed value on every house, apartment, business, or other structure in Columbia goes into the Association's treasury. It exercises a first lien on all property in Columbia which supercedes any other obligations, even taking precedence over Federal Housing Authority (FHA) and Veteran's Administration (VA) mortgage claims. Thus the economic base of the Columbia Association is grounded in the bedrock of the community and cannot radically change, though its income is, of course, subject to external factors such as property evaluation levels, population growth, and the general economic well being of the nation.[1]

Within the framework of activities operated by the Columbia Association, it has been possible to arrange for a kind of subsidization of certain human services, such as day care, rather than putting the entire burden on the

[1]It should be noted that other new towns which have since tried to install a similar system of financing the management of their communities unfortunately found both the VA and FHA unwilling to surrender their first claims as home mortgagers. This policy shift has made it more difficult for such communities to devise a viable scheme for financing the management of crucial facilities. It is apparent that in this country the development of any new community is tied up unavoidably with federal policies in a vast number of respects having not only to do with difficulties in financing such projects without government loan guarantees but also bearing on the kinds of people who can be accommodated and the nature of human needs that can be met. A tragic instance is the inability of new town developers to provide low-income housing and thus ensure a socially desirable population mix following the Nixon administration's decision to set aside almost all programs of housing assistance.

immediate consumers of those services. All profits from commercial facilities operated by the Columbia Association, such as the ice rink, the year-round swimming pool, and the golf courses, are combined with other income to the Association, which also operates loss operations such as the day-care programs. In this way the Association is able to support certain human services that could not fully fund themselves on a straight fee for service basis while remaining available to all those in need of them, including low-income residents.

FACILITATING DEVELOPMENT OF OTHER INSTITUTIONS

A difficult task had been the planning of space for non-existent institutions, the nature of which could not be known until settlement was well underway and space already allocated. How could the social planner know, once the initial list had been run through, what kinds of institutions were about to spring up by residents' or outside initiative, and how they would be taken care of if they did? One solution has been to include within each village center spaces that could be used for emerging institutions. Generally, into the office areas of the centers have been built comparatively low-rent space for use by local or other groups wishing to locate in the village. In Columbia's first village, such space was put to good use by a number of groups, among them Grassroots and the first counseling office of the Family Life Center, described elsewhere in this issue. Such flexible, low-priced office space also has proved useful for national special interest groups, many of whom exist on limited budgets and are not assured permanent financial support. It has been the responsibility of the institutional development team to see that space is available for such institutions, to assist in development, and to help them deal with the rest of the developer's corporate structure, most notably marketing and sales.

ENCOURAGING INITIATIVE IN INSTITUTIONAL DEVELOPMENT

However much of it might be rationalized after the fact, Columbia's social development process—beyond the basic minimum of health, education, recreation, and day-care services—took place for the most part on an ad hoc basis. No comprehensive presettlement scheme was articulated that set forth the nature of the social institutions, the timing of their development, and the economic considerations to be noted. Once settlement began there was no mechanism, either within the Association or any other agency, for providing systematic assessment of needs, initiation of programs, and monitoring of services. The developer was reticent—as, indeed, are most new town entrepreneurs—to remain at the center of social-institutional planning. The dilemma is how to provide a means for comprehensive coordination of human services without inducing undue dependence on and undemocratic control by the developer. Columbia's answer was to adopt a kind of modified, bright idea marketplace approach which has had the distinct advantage of encouraging initiative and control of residents from the outset. It has also allowed programs to emerge, others to be modified, still others to flourish and later disappear in response to changing and often unpredictable needs and conditions in the ever-enlarging community. It has the obvious disadvantage of not being able to identify unmet needs with any degree of certainty or to foresee emerging areas of need with an optimal amount of lead time. One result is that the institutional development team is left with few criteria for determining which of the many budding institutions to support and which to ignore or possibly even discourage. The tendency has been to try to provide as much breathing space as possible for virtually any new idea. On the positive side, such a strategy has meant that even those schemes which seemed outlandish at the outset have sometimes worked out and gained solid community support over time.

SEEDING THE DEVELOPMENT PROCESS

Once the community enters the settlement phase, certain elements seem to be highly desirable for creative institutional development: (1) one or more persons responsible primarily for institutional development whose job it is to encourage the emerging interests and concerns within the community and to welcome initiatives from outside organizations; (2) the provision of low-cost space for use by newly emerging groups; (3) some sort of seed money which can be used to support promising undertakings by residents and others in their initial stages.

A major question that immediately presents itself is who should be providing the needed seed funds for community development. Few new communities have the basis of wealth among its initial residents to do so. It is probably unwise to make such seeding dependent on the developer, who is then in a position to have a disproportionate influence over social-institutional development. A mechanism is needed that will set the community free to make sound policy judgments about community needs and priorities. The Columbia Foundation was established as such a mechanism. It is an independent funding agency with its own community board which administers and disburses funds collected from business firms and individual givers. Stimulated by the developer, the Foundation secured a modest but continuing financial base from the first bank in Columbia which, at the developer's suggestion, agreed to allocate 10 percent of its profits each year to the Foundation. This initial pool of money has since been enlarged through other contributions. It is used to stimulate and sustain the early efforts of community groups seeking to launch promising social programs.

GAINING CREDIBILITY FOR THE SOCIAL PLANNER

The Columbia experience suggests that it is essential for social planners to establish credibility within the developmental team if institutional development is to proceed on a sound basis. Social planners have found it exceedingly difficult to establish such credibility because few ways have been found to relate their activities directly to the economic productivity of an undertaking. This problem was reduced somewhat in Columbia when the institutional development function was placed within the marketing division. The institutional development representative was given a portfolio of activity which included both social concerns and certain commercial development as well, with the intent of ensuring that his total productivity would match or exceed the cost of his activities. In this manner, he has gained considerable internal credibility both for himself and for the social concerns for which he is responsible. Historically, the social planner in new towns has been a kind of hair shirt or bleeding heart within community development whose proposals were frequently overruled for political and economic reasons. By gaining credibility within the important marketing function of Columbia, the social planner was able to communicate more effectively within the planning team and tended to incorporate in his considerations matters having to do with economics (such as the income to be gained from a particular land use as versus other alternatives) as well as the social benefits to be realized.

ECONOMICS OF INSTITUTIONAL DEVELOPMENT

With hindsight, it is easy to see that a kind of unrealistic optimism can occur with a new town such as Columbia, which is prepared to invest major time and effort in imaginative institutional planning. The result is that in some cases very mundane marketplace considerations are overlooked, and there is a contagion of mutual reinforcement among the institutional developers and those seeking to establish their dream in the new town. Some efforts which failed to take root in the early years, when altogether too few individuals were living in Columbia, might have been postponed to a more suitable time when the population base might have warranted them; others might never have been attempted at all if advice had been sought from economic experts on the development team. It is clear that institutional development within the free enterprise system requires a unique combination of two qualities: (1) a sense of economic discipline and (2) a willingness to think innovatively. Those projects which have done well are those for which the institutional development team did its economic homework, in effect saying, "Here's a good idea; how are we going to make it work out financially" rather than "Here's a good idea which must work just because it is so appealing."

Without an adequate economic plan, failure of a good idea is altogether too likely. And when social institutions fail, the effect can be far more devastating than a business failure. One consequence is the reluctance of the same or similar external institutions to try again even when conditions are more favorable. There is, in the first place, only a limited set of external institutions capable of making the effort in any single area of social need. When one tries unsuccessfully to innovate something in the new town, its management and community policy boards will not be easily persuaded to make another try. Business institutions are successful only within a climate of realistic risk taking. Social institutions, on the other hand, are rarely oriented to a risk mentality, dependent as they are on charitable or tax dollars. They usually lack venture capital or the mechanisms for securing it. Yet there must be the capacity to take risk if institutional development is to be attempted in new towns and such risks must be taken both by the new institution and its sponsors and by the developer, who in turn must be prepared to invest time, effort, and money in a social engineering process long before ultimate economic or social payoffs become apparent.

It is clear from the foregoing that a fundamental problem in new town development involves a continuous strain between social and economic values, which at times come into sharp conflict with one another. A successful program of institutional development requires the person or persons charged with the responsibility for this phase of new town development to maintain an acute sensitivity to these strains and to deal with them in a creative way.

9. From Counterculture Self-Help to Community Self-Help

ALLAN FEINSTEIN

Grassroots, located in the new town of Columbia, Maryland, is one of the hundreds of peer-style help centers started in the late 1960's and early 1970's as an alternative community mental health approach to youth problems and drug abuse. Four years and six staff generations later, it has evolved into a more comprehensive, stable, and sophisticated program that is still operating a walk-in counseling center, a hotline, and an emergency outreach service allowing staff to go to the scene of a mental health crisis.

I have written this article from the perspective of a clinical, community psychologist who has been serving as the organization's executive director for eight months. It has been an intriguing period fraught with challenging dilemmas and opportunities as the program walks the line between becoming a more established alternative agency and becoming another agency of the establishment.[1]

For me, the most striking realization about Grassroots has been that the primary self help and humanistic values about human service stated formally and behaviorally by

[1]See *A Hotline Cools Off* by Killeen & Schmitz (1973) for a description of the pitfalls of "making it" as an alternative agency.

74

the organization's counterculture forebearers—young, radical, and hip—have stayed intact in the agency's evolution into a more established program staffed by older (average age just under 30), middle-class types who are less radical in life-style but who more closely reflect the community of which they are a part. I also believe that the values which have survived the organization's transmutations bear a marked resemblance to principles articulated by community psychologists for developing the "competent community" (Iscoe, 1974), especially those emphasizing preventive and educational human service approaches geared toward citizens competent in meeting human needs, peer-help, and self-help.

HISTORY[2]

Grassroots was opened in August 1970 by a group of Antioch College[3] students and their friends, with active support and collaboration by the Howard County Mental Health Association, the new town's developer, the Maryland State Department of Health and Mental Hygiene, and several local citizens and professionals. The original staff reflected many of the earmarks and values of the counterculture movement: unshorn appearance, personally sophisticated in the use of illicit drugs, and deeply concerned with social injustice, cosmic consciousness, and a "reaching out to our brothers and sisters" ethic.

[2]Sources include a descriptive investigation and evaluation of the program commissioned by the funding source and conducted by an applied anthropologist (Lennhoff, 1971), a study of Grassroots by a team from the Joint Information Service of the American Psychiatric Association and the National Association for Mental Health which was investigating alternative treatment programs (Glasscote, et al., 1975), other documents in Grassroots' files, interviews, and personal observations.
[3]Antioch College, whose main campus is in Yellow Springs, Ohio, had established a satellite campus in Columbia.

The organization's objectives in its original application for funds were "To provide an informal counseling setting in which youth will have an opportunity to discuss and seek to understand their problems with drugs, and to explore possible alternatives" (Lennhoff, 1971). From the beginning, many non-drug-related calls were also received, and after two months the organization's objectives were expanded to include dealing with problems involving family, school, pregnancy, birth control, draft, loneliness, and "other personal concerns." In addition, the organization attempted, with limited success, to provide such activities as arts, crafts, drama, yoga, and discussion groups. More successful were outreach workers who frequented concerts, a lakefront, and other gathering places for large numbers of youth for the purpose of providing immediate crisis intervention and counseling. Numerous "bad trips" and drug overdoses received an immediate response through this service.

The program's first annual budget was in the vicinity of $80,000, most of it provided by the State Department of Mental Hygiene as a demonstration grant. Other contributions were also received, and Columbia's developer donated rent-free space. This substantial funding base allowed for a 14-person staff on subsistence wages to operate the center 24 hours daily. These counterculture counselors were, at best, casual in their fiscal administration procedures: keeping virtually no usable records during the first six months of operation, not withholding taxes, not producing receipts for expenditures, taking the liberty to provide clients with "loans" for abortions, bail, and other personal crises, and the expectation of being paid regardless of whether they came into work or "just couldn't get it together" for a while. To the counselors, these deviations from normal fiscal management seemed consistent with their values and life-styles, but they were a source of considerable consternation to the community and funding sources.

The entire program was greeted with marked ambivalence in the community. On the one hand, residents were very concerned with youth problems and drug abuse, and there was growing evidence that Grassroots' peer-counselors were able to establish rapport and help individuals who could not be reached by other mental health services. On the other hand, their unwashed appearance and counterculture life-styles set an example that was upsetting for many. Runaways and drug abusers were given support for their feelings rather than admonishment that their behavior was wrong, which may have been good counseling, but was infuriating to many parents. In addition, the program was housed in a new office building which the staff maintained in a sorry state and which was frequented by "assorted dogs and overnight crashers;" another tenant of the building moved out in protest (Lennhoff, 1971). Grassroots "feasts," a short-lived Monday night program which invited everyone in the community for a free spaghetti dinner and a sense of community, was publicized in a widely distributed flier that announced with wide-eyed enthusiasm: "Free dinner Monday ... bring food if you have it, instruments if you play them, come together, eat, drink, sing, dance, live, breathe, fuck, dig everybody and rap about it." The flier became notorious, and its language received far wider press than did the event it announced, leaving a mark on the organization's image that four years later has not been erased completely.

Nonetheless, Grassroots was able to maintain community support, especially from a committed group of citizens organized as "Friends of Grassroots" and a small but active Board of Directors which buffered, guided, and provided continuity from one staff to the next. Staff members were highly committed, often working in excess of 80 hours weekly, but Grassroots staffs had short half-lives. In discussing why the founding group either left the program or had given notification that they were leaving before the agency was a year old, Lennhoff (1971) observed:

> It is not uncommon for the founders of a program to become dissatisfied once it is running. The dynamism which makes it possible to be a pioneer often becomes dysfunctional if a program is to run smoothly . . . . Some of the "old-timers" were incompetent and they have left. Others have become exhausted or burned out by the stressful work. Still others wish Grassroots would be a vehicle for innovative community organization. It can't be, and they shall leave.

But the founders were replaced by a new group which had its own start-up crises requiring pioneering and dynamism, and the Grassroots staff remained a highly committed group with life-style and organizational style intertwined—working hard, burning itself out to be replaced by a new group. Each successive staff, however, inherited a history, competencies, and procedures from the previous generation, so that as the organization evolved, its sophistication increased.

While Grassroots still had a hip and radical appearance in 1973, an increasingly large percentage of volunteer counselors were college graduates who held positions of responsibility in their respective professions. Grassroots became a starting place for many staff members to enter the mental health professions—for some this involved changing a major in college, for others it involved major career changes. Housewives found the organization a good starting point in personal redefinition of societal function. As staff evolved away from a core counterculture group, so did clientele—these shifts reflecting, at least in part, changes within both the community and the country. Drug "freakout" calls began to be replaced by an increasing percentage of mental health focused problems. The average age of staff and clients increased, signaling greater respectability for the agency in the community among older individuals who were willing to become involved with the organization in both roles.

Despite the increases in age of staff and clientele (in 1973, 50% of the clients were 20 or older), the organization remained a major youth-serving group as attested to by a National Institute of Mental Health-funded survey by CoRAL,II, Columbia's Community Research and Action Laboratory. This survey reports that teenagers in Columbia who were polled on what resources they would turn to for help with personal problems mentioned Grassroots more than three times as frequently as any other service (Klein, Karsk, & Weiss, 1974). Nonetheless, the "youth owned and operated" atmosphere disappeared.

More and more, the staff was able to present a responsible image to the community. By 1974, a study team interested in alternative treatment approaches headed by Raymond Glasscote, Chief of the Joint Information Service of the American Psychiatric Association and the National Association for Mental Health, found Grassroots to be a "remarkably organized, systematic, and professionally sound program that has evolved from its original founding group of extraordinarily counterculture types" (Glasscote, Raybin, & Reifler, 1975).

The Joint Information Service report (Glasscote, *et al.,* 1975) raises the question of whether Grassroots, as it has evolved, has been able to maintain itself as an alternative service, and concludes that "To question the alternative nature of Grassroots is to suggest that all services provided in a systematic and informed way are by definition *traditional* or *professional* ... Grassroots is an alternative service by virtue of its policy of accepting all who come, serving them promptly, keeping them out of trouble-fraught official hands such as the police whenever possible, charging no fees, and referring them, when the problem is beyond the agency's competence, to another agency with more specific or intensive skills."

Grassroots has, in fact, remained highly conscious of

sustaining an alternative approach which includes providing an immediate response to client needs in an informal setting which involves a great deal of individual, personalized attention and caring. Appointments are not required, there are no delays due to complex intake procedures, there is no waiting list, services are provided at unusual hours, and staff can go to the scene of a mental health emergency to do crisis intervention work.

Despite these virtues, funding did not come easily after the renewable demonstration grant exhausted its two-year limit. The fiscal year 1974 budget was only $24,000, less than one-third the original funding. Problems with fiscal support over the years had affected the program in a variety of ways, including staff burn-out, and finally forcing the agency to reduce its hours from 24 round-the-clock service to 6 or 7 hours daily.

BEHAVIORAL SCIENTIST AS EXECUTIVE DIRECTOR

Grassroots' fifth executive director—long-haired, bearded, and, like his predecessors, generally counterculture in style and appearance—decided to leave the program in April, 1974. The organization by that time seemed to be in perpetual crisis with its drastically reduced funding base, decreased service hours (a striking disadvantage to a crisis intervention center), its volunteer staff burning out rapidly, low morale, resentment toward the community for not providing greater support, and a recent announcement from the new town developer that it would be unable to continue subsidizing the program with free space after the end of the fiscal year. Despite these misfortunes, the Board and staff appeared amazingly undaunted and optimistic about the organization's future. Such commitment and faith have, in fact, seemed key ingredients to the organization's tenacity over the years.

I personally had been involved periodically with Grassroots from its early days when I served as an outside organizational consultant and trainer to the first staff.[4] I worked in a similar capacity with a subsequent staff generation and employed members of still a third staff in developing a statewide training program for crisis intervention counselors. I had not worked with the staff that existed in April, 1974, but in assessing the organization at that time I noted that while the program was clearly in the most desperate financial state in its history, the paid staff remaining with Grassroots was composed of two remarkably talented, vastly underpaid committed individuals. The 10-member volunteer staff was also an incredibly rich and competent group of people. What the organization lacked in physical resources, it made up for in talent, spirit, and determination to provide the community with an alternative, person-to-person, round-the-clock, peer-help approach to community mental health.

The vacancy in the executive director position was intriguing to me. I was interested in finding ways that the knowledge and competencies of behavioral sciences could be passed on to citizens, groups, and organizations for improving the quality of life in their community (Feinstein and Spencer, 1971; Miller, 1969). If the fiscal and organizational problems could be overcome, it appeared that Grassroots could be an excellent base for a clinical, community psychologist with my interests.

Despite warnings from friends and colleagues that overcoming the forces of impending fiscal disaster might overshadow any more idealistic aspirations, I applied for and was offered the $7,000 per year directorship from a field of 30 applicants (most of whom withdrew upon learning of the salary).

I enjoyed a brief honeymoon of some 30 minutes with Grassroots. I had worked out a way to immediately bring resources into the program to cover my salary and made it a condition of my accepting the position that the excess

[4]I was at the time a staff member of the NTL-Community Research and Action Laboratory which was located in Columbia between 1970 and 1971 and which spawned CoRAL,II (cited earlier).

funds go into hiring a full-time administrative assistant so that my commitment could be limited to three days per week. This arrangement made it financially feasible for me to take the job while allowing me to continue some teaching and clinical work. The Board agreed to this proposal with the understanding that it would be evaluated after three months to determine if it was functional.

The volunteer staff, on the other hand, was furious that the Board had agreed to such significant organization changes without first having consulted them. They made their dissatisfaction very clear immediately at a staff meeting which was occurring in a room adjacent to the Board meeting where I was being formally hired. Two especially sensitive areas included volunteer staff's feelings that they were losing control of the organization's destiny, which had always been in counseling staff hands, and the fact that because I had a doctorate, the staff suspected that special concessions were being made to me in order to bring this credibility device into the organization. Grassroots had already lost its counterculture flavor, and staff feared that, in its struggle to survive, its identity as an alternative service would also be sacrificed.

Partially because of the credibility I had gained in my work with previous Grassroots staffs, volunteers tended to accept me, but at the same time they strongly resented my Ph.D., which represented another step away from the citizen-run, unprofessionalized, peer-help program that Grassroots had always been. My coming on staff also seemed to symbolize the transition from peer-style management to an organization with functional role differentiations. For some time the staff had felt the dilemma that they could be either a good family or a good counseling service, but it was difficult to be both. The option of remaining a family no longer existed, as my mandate included increasing the volunteer counseling staff from 10 to 50 as a means of resuming 24-hour service. Previously about 14 paid and volunteer staff members were able to keep the organization open 24 hours while managing it somewhat like a family, but funding cutbacks forced services to be reduced to 6 hours daily making a large volunteer staff necessary if round-the-clock crisis intervention services were to be reestablished. Although this necessity eliminated the possibility of a family-like organization, I often felt that the staff's deep ambivalence about losing this possibility was symbolized in me and their resentment manifested itself in a variety of ways.

I vividly recall one meeting soon after I started the job that lasted well beyond 2 A.M. in which everything I was doing seemed unacceptable to at least some staff members. I began by trying to help facilitate the very confusing session and quickly learned that, in my new role, I could not use the organization development skills that had been so useful in working as a consultant with previous Grassroots staffs. Each of the conditions I had set in taking the job was attacked: my insistence on an administrative assistant was putting too much emphasis on administration when the program was hurting desperately; my interest in accepting a purchase of service contract to expand services in new areas was evidence of my ambition to build an empire; my concern with documentation and community image was seen as professionalism; my 3-day per week work arrangement made my level of commitment dubious to this highly committed group of volunteers; my previous connections with the local health department were viewed with suspicion that I was hoping to make Grassroots an extension of that more traditional service; my unashamed use of the Ph.D. was seen as an attempt to mask the peer-level counseling approach with a more professional image while also trying to one-up the staff; my ability to locate funding to cover my salary was met with general distrust that I was pulling strings somewhere. In brief, I felt quite lonely in the early days of my new job with Grassroots.

Some of the distrust has been erased by time and acquaintance. Some lifted after behavioral demonstration of high commitment on my part both to the organization and to its stance as an alternative agency. The most powerful factor in my coming to be accepted by the counseling staff, however, rests in the fact that Grassroots has trained and accepted some 30 new volunteer counselors in the 8 months since I took the job, and I now find myself increasingly in the early settler's position—feeling concerned that *they* do not understand Grassroots' history and the significance of remaining a truly alternative agency. My initiation as executive director was an important part of my education for effectively utilizing these feelings when working with new staff members.

CONTINUING CRISIS CENTER CRISES

From the first day I occupied the "executive suite," an eight by ten foot office shared by the four full-time staff members, a couch, two chairs, supplies, literature, files, a 1929 Royal typewriter, and two desks, Grassroots was faced with a host of pressing crisis situations. The counterculture drug image was becoming costly as drug monies dried up, and the community's discomfort was further fanned by internal conflicts made public and unpopular stands on controversial issues proclaimed publicly by some former staff members. Nine months earlier the community had stood by without intervening when Grassroots was forced to severely reduce its service hours from round-the-clock (which a handful of people had been heroically maintaining for some time) to evenings only. Community support became even harder to sustain after that with the decrease in service hours and visibility and fewer staff members available for community organization and public relations. The evidence indicated that the community would allow the organization to die, as it had already done with two other hard-working, committed, innovative youth programs and a well-liked community self-help organization called Friendship Exchange. The developer announced that the free rent could not be con-

tinued, the state informed the program that it was un-
likely that drug monies could be maintained even at their
current level, and other outside funding sources for such
programs had also rapidly diminished. It seemed clear
that, in order to survive, Grassroots would have to simultaneously double or triple its revenues, radically improve
its community image and support base, expand volunteer
counseling staff and service hours with no increased program funds, and efficiently, effectively, and competently
function and adapt during this intense period of transition.

Still staff and Board were optimistic and forward-think-
ing, and progress began to be achieved in each of the
areas critical for survival. The program staff was talented;
their 40-hour intensive counselor training program,
which is followed by an apprenticeship, attracted over
100 people in a 6-month period, 30 of whom have become
qualified counselors, each volunteering in excess of 10
hours weekly. Over two-thirds of the volunteers held
Bachelors degrees; one-third had Masters. The training
received wide community recognition with various local
leaders wishing to participate, adding to Grassroots' credibility. Other organizations asked Grassroots to provide
training to their staffs. Johns Hopkins University, Antioch
College, the University of Maryland, and Loyola College
all offered course credit or field placements to students
who went through the training program and became volunteers.

With increased involvement of competent citizens, the
job of improving the organization's community image
became easier. My activity in the community was extensive and calculated. At first, I would often be met with the
opinion that Grassroots was a self-serving group of hippies
deeply involved in the drug culture. In a meeting with the
county's high school principals, my claims that the organization had changed were countered with the observation that it was always changing and nothing I could say
was going to get them to open their schools to Grassroots

counselors. After several similar encounters with the establishment I began to mention my degree to mildly surprised community leaders, carried hand-outs indicating a profile of Grassroots volunteer counselors, and postponed plans to cultivate a beard. Slowly but steadily, a broader and broader segment of the community came to see Grassroots as a legitimate counseling resource.

A big break came when the United Fund of Central Maryland, deciding that the program was worthy of saving and restoring to 24-hour service, allocated $26,220 for Fiscal Year 1975, beginning two and one-half months after I assumed the directorship. Money begets money: the Board was able to convince the county that it should match the United Fund's investment in Grassroots, and with their decision to allocate $17,342 to the program, survival was assured, and I let my beard bloom freely.

As successes started to mount, the state agency charged with accrediting counseling programs such as Grassroots dealt a crippling blow by withdrawing the program's license to operate based on allegations that Grassroots staff, Board, and friends felt were fabricated and outrageous. The reasons for the attack were not apparent, but it was suspected by some that they involved political retaliation to a county that has twice organized public support to stand up against this state agency. Regardless of the reasons, Grassroots again was in a crisis with all energy mobilized to have certification restored (paid staff each averaged 80 hours per week during part of this period). The recent community organization work suddenly became a critical asset. After an incredibly difficult, frustrating, demoralizing month of frenetic but politically astute activity on Grassroots' part, the State agency was forced to reverse its position and admit that "Grassroots is doing a commendable job." This victory served as a rite of passage, and after recovering from the battle, the staff has been able to attend to the job of building a sound organization around a rapidly growing program.

GRASSROOTS GROWING

As Grassroots is approaching its immediate goal of providing 24-hour crisis intervention and counseling services, some critical questions are emerging. The rapid increase in volunteer staff poses the dilemma that it is difficult to maintain a broad base of ownership and individual influence in the larger organization. The ownership and commitment of the founding Grassroots staff was inherent with their life-styles being intimately intertwined with the small organization. Grassroots is now adjunct, rather than central, to the life-styles of most volunteer staff members and payment is in terms of satisfying work, meaningful activity, channels for acting on values and ideals, increased competence in human service and personal growth skills, a means for serving the community, and association with an enriching organization and group of people. While these attractions do account for the high commitment a large number of people have for Grassroots, shared ownership among staff members is no longer automatic as it had been when Grassroots was a life-style as well as a good place to volunteer.

Grassroots has been experimenting with an emergent representative management style which promises to significantly increase the individual counselor's impact on the organization's decision making and direction. Each counselor's case supervision and in-service training is conducted in core groups with five or six other counselors and a supervisor who meet on a weekly basis utilizing both peer and professional supervision and training in an atmosphere of trust, intimacy, and commitment to competent, human responses to client needs. The core groups serve as the counselors' basic support system as well as a basic political unit. A representative from each core group serves with the four paid staff members as part of a management team which functionally does have executive ownership of Grassroots.

Related to maintaining broad staff ownership is the

unending challenge of keeping Grassroots a vital, exciting, and renewing organization. In many ways, it is by
virtue of these qualities that the agency is such a potent
alternative to more traditional mental health services.
Developing a vital, nonbureaucratic, shared-manage-
ment organization is one key to maintaining such excitement. More important, however, is the fact that
Grassroots counselors are local residents who are there for
the purpose of providing help to their neighbors, which
injects their work with an enthusiasm and willingness to
extend themselves that has healing properties in itself.
This stance in tandem with their ability to create Rogers'
(1957) "necessary and sufficient conditions" of a helping
relationship, as selected lay people can rapidly be taught
to do (Carkhuff, 1969), all combines into a powerful service.

Citizens who want to work with Grassroots and are not
inclined to serve as counselors are reorganizing Friends of
Grassroots, which had folded in 1972. This auxiliary organization will support Board and staff in diverse ways,
ranging from fund-raising to publicity to locating individuals willing to provide emergency overnight housing to
building a large membership base. The large membership
will be oriented toward peer-help in the community and
will provide grass roots citizen investment and ownership
in the Grassroots program.

The future holds exciting challenges for a growing
Grassroots program geared to promoting peer-help and
self-help responses to human needs in Howard County. As
veteran volunteers have reached the point of having
learned most of the skills Grassroots is likely to offer them,
they have tended to move on from the agency. While the
organization viewed such "graduations" as successes in
that the community's base-level of helping skills among
citizens was increased in the process, these more experienced volunteer counselors are now being seen as a tre-
mendous resource which can be attracted to stay with

Grassroots if given more advanced training in the exciting behavioral science frontiers being developed for self-help and personal growth (Feinstein, 1971). Plans are underway to design a training program in group processes for advanced Grassroots counselors to enable them to skillfully conduct rap groups, counseling groups, and experiential educational events. Staff members with such competencies could be involved in community outreach and education working in a variety of topic areas such as communication, personal identity, interpersonal skills, self-management, family dynamics, parent enabling, intergenerational issues, assertiveness training, life planning, achievement motivation, self-concept enhancement, and values clarification in such areas as drugs, sex, and career choice. Because Grassroots staff is citizen-based, the agency is able to work with systems in ways professionals cannot. Early indications suggest the community would seek Grassroots outreach and education programs, and the potent tools available for implementing such programs could give the organization powerful momentum for furthering its mission of utilizing an educational approach to mental health for promoting peer-help and self-help in Howard County.

REFERENCES

Carkhuff, R. R. *Helping and human relations: a primer for lay and professional helpers. Volume 1: selection and training. Volume 2: practice and research.* New York: Holt, Rinehart and Winston, 1969.

Feinstein, A. (Ed.) *Readings in applied behavioral science —part I: personal growth.* Baltimore: Maryland State Department of Health and Mental Hygiene, 1971.

Feinstein, A. & Spencer, M. *Technical innovation in applied behavioral science.* Baltimore: Maryland State Department of Health and Mental Hygiene, 1971.

Glasscote, R. M., Raybin, J. E., & Reifler, C. *Alternative Services—Their Role in Mental Health.* Washington, D.C.: Joint Information Service, 1975.

Iscoe, I. Community psychology and the competent community. *American Psychologist,* 1974, *29*(8), 607–613.

Killeen, M. & Schmitz, M. A hotline cools off. *Personnel and Guidance Journal,* 1973, *52*(4), 250–252.

Klein, D., Karsk, R., and Weiss, J. Working paper no. 2: a survey of new town teenagers' activities and usage of facilities, part I—analysis of teens' responses. *Developed by CoRAL,II, the Community Research and Action Laboratory as part of NIMH Grant #MH23664-01, 1974.*

Lennhoff, S. *Community mental health studies No. I: a descriptive evaluation of Grassroots.* Baltimore: Maryland State Department of Health and Mental Hygiene, 1971.

Miller, G. Psychology as a means of promoting human welfare. *American Psychologist,* 1969, *24*, 1063–1075.

Rogers, C.R. The necessary and sufficient conditions of therapeutic personality change. *Journal of Consulting Psychology,* 1957, *21*, 95–103.

10.   A New Mental Health Delivery Model in a New City

LYNN SHOFFEITT
PAUL SHOFFEITT

Set between two urban cosmopolitan centers the community of Columbia has attracted many people for whom mental health is a sought-after commodity. The influx of these people during Columbia's development occurred in a time characterized by an unpopular war, dramatically changing mores, corruption in government, energy shortages combined with high unemployment and inflation and at least temporary disruption of the nuclear family. A community less averse to seeking professional mental health services and one which has felt profoundly the political, economic, and cultural reverberations that have troubled the nation compounded to put more stress on the limited mental health services that had previously been available for a more pastoral, family-centered, and low density county. The improbability of attracting a comprehensive community mental health grant during the years of diminishing federal funding called for an inventiveness born of necessity.

In the midst of one of the busiest marketplaces in Columbia, between the Cheese Shop and an ice cream parlor, lies the Family Life Center, an unpretentious, highly innovative mental health resource that may serve as a

91

stimulating model for imaginative, low-cost, high-yield programs elsewhere. From its storefront through its open space to its philosophical moorings this organization defies the usual stigma associated with the seeking of more traditional mental health services.

On any day, within its vibrant yellow and orange walls papered with community bulletins, one may find people chatting, volunteers orienting visitors to the self-help files and libraries, and children playing around a toy bin. A warm ambience pervades the room, inviting people to partake of its offerings.

What lies behind this pleasant picture? The scene symbolizes the marriage of the concepts of several behavioral scientists and social-minded entrepreneurs. From the earliest work group days preceding Columbia, there was a general awareness of the emotional needs of families who would populate this new town. The original designers were committed to some kind of resource center for such families. For several years, this idea lay dormant awaiting its moment in the evolution of the city.

Then, through a small initial grant from a local foundation and interest of the new town developer, a Family Life Institute was created to offer preventive mental health programs to the community. These programs included such resources as family communications courses, effective parenting classes, and similar educational opportunities that could support families in all their stages.

Columbia began attracting large numbers of mental health professionals as residents, more than the average town its size and much like university communities such as Berkeley and Ann Arbor. Many of these professionals, most of whom are employed by the surrounding urban centers of Baltimore, the District of Columbia, and the wealthier, more developed bedroom communities of Prince George's and Montgomery Counties that have received the outward sprawl from the District, were drawn to Columbia as a unique home for themselves and their families. The Center is dedicated primarily to providing treatment services and preventive education, and secondarily to supporting other sources of mental health wherever they are found in the community.

The idea of utilizing this treasury of professionals in such a way as to alleviate the overwhelming demands for counseling services germinated among several behavioral scientists in Columbia. Their idea was to recruit local professionals to work during off hours and provide a second source of counseling services out of an altruistic concern for the community on a semi-volunteer basis. By maintaining a low overhead, the administration of such services were streamlined to help meet the staggering number of requests being made on the traditional mental health services in the county. These two organizations Family Life Institute and the Personal and Family Consultation Service shared a similar philosophy and the same rich pool of professional resources; as the months passed, it became a very natural step to merge the two into one entity, the Family Life Center. Half unwittingly, the originators had tapped a little-used human resource: the *indigenous professional.* Community psychologists, who traditionally have been fond of finding the hidden talents in nonprofessionals, can appreciate this twist; the Family Life Center had tapped the wealth of the volunteer clinical community as well as the skills of the lay community.

After the first professional recruits began the services, the counseling ranks continued to swell. Other professionals began to *seek* this new avenue of service, causing a growth that far exceeded the dreams of the originators. Unanticipated resources, e.g., retired therapists and professional women who had temporarily left the job market to raise young children, joined the counseling pool. Running the gamut of the mental health professions, they represented an exciting breadth and depth of training and experience to give the community *and* share with each other. Their motives have gone beyond the simple desire to give community service, extending to the search for more colleagueship, continued professional training, and the opportunity to work in a more flexible structure.

The use of such an array of talent is a coordinator's dream come true. As a client seeks counseling help, the intake person does not merely rely on whoever has an open hour in a busy schedule as is the case in the usual agency. Rather, she is challenged to be selective, linking the presenting need of the client to the specific skills or interests of a particular counselor. The 75 counselors on the Family Life Center roster represent such specialties as behavior therapy, family therapy, play therapy, gestalt, transactional analysis, marriage counseling, adolescent identity counseling, vocational counseling, and child evaluations. In addition, several psychiatrists are available for medical back-up and consultation. A panel of active psychotherapists from the Center's Board of Directors set the criteria of training and experience and personally screen counselors before accepting them on the Center's roster.

In the area of preventive programming, the Family Life Center has expanded on the work of its forerunner institute to provide programs that will give people tools for coping with their own lives, prevent debilitating crises, and reduce demand on the mental health network for treatment services. These programs include a spectrum of groups in parent education and family communications, transactional analysis, marriage enrichment, activity therapy groups for youngsters, and adult-teenager relations.

The educational programs and their leaders are carefully screened by a committee from the Board of Directors to assure high quality, low cost preventive programs. The positive format in which they are publicized to the community further enhances a favorable image of mental health.

The dynamic quality of growth within the organization keeps pace with the same quality in the larger community. The Center's synergistic character makes its true size hard to measure at any moment, and requires constant reassessment by staff and Board. All of the services are guided by the Board and administered by a small, mostly part-time, paid staff of only five people.

The interaction between the Board and staff, counselors, group leaders, volunteers, and community represents an interesting model of accountability. Each Board member, selected to reflect the diversity of the County, works on at least one and usually two, committees. Literally hundreds of hours have been volunteered by the Board, working on such committees as Philosophy and Goals Task Force, Personnel, Counselor Screening, Program Screening, Finance, and Evaluation Task Force. A Committee on Board Functioning assures the continual reevaluation of the Board's and, thus, the organization's effectiveness. The Committees' deliberations stimulate and guide the continuing evolution of the Family Life Center's philosophy, objectives, and machinery.

The responsibilities and work of the Family Life Center are thus diffused among the working Board, the small paid staff, and professional and lay volunteers. A great deal of trust is imperative in such a system, creating a strong sense of ownership by the persons who give of themselves within the Center. For lack of a better term, we have called this organizational structure a "circular model," where people are responsible to themselves and each other and ultimately to the larger community. As in other circular models, ideas are spawned and spun off as a result of centrifugal force. We see the Family Life Center at its best as not only delivering the core services of counseling and education, but also facilitating new ideas that eventually have a life of their own within the community, some of them quite apart from the Center itself.

One such good idea grew from the very location of the physical facility. Because of its visibility and accessibility, not to mention our ambiguous name, people began to call and drop by to ask for all kinds of information. It was a logical move to begin gathering information to meet these requests. Several community women, some of whom were representing groups, decided to unite to amass information specifically, but not exclusively, for women. The Women's Resource Center was thus born. Its volunteers soon began to staff our Center during weekday office hours and Saturday. An independent organization, yet cooperatively utilizing our space for mutual benefit, they have produced such projects as a separation and divorce crisis handbook and a vocational counseling center.

Other spin-offs, which might not have been possible within a more rigid structure, have included a popular periodic group for newly divorced or separated people, a peer counseling training program for people experiencing sudden physical disabilities, a home/health-aide program, a minister's counseling training program, and a cooperative effort to obtain comprehensive mental health funding for the entire county. Preventive mental health columns in two local newspapers are coordinated by the Family Life Center. They draw from the storehouse of local professional expertise; as a preventive and educational tool, these two columns reach over half the homes in the community.

A key element in the success of the Family Life Center is the effort to build a mutually rewarding exchange system. Recognizing that people typically give in proportion to what they receive, be it monetary, additional skills, a feeling of service, or an opportunity to see their own ideas take shape, we have attempted to build those reinforcements into our circular model. For example, while very talented professionals give their time for minimal fees, they have an opportunity for monthly training functions where fellow counselors teach their specialties, e.g., Gestalt, Psychodrama, Structural Patterning, Behavior or Family Therapies. Once a year, nationally known persons of the caliber of family therapists Jay Haley and Virginia Satir bring a major workshop experience.

Aside from the resource which the Family Life Center represents to this particular community, its model for the delivery of human services has implications beyond Columbia and Howard County. One of the hopes of new towns is that these planned communities will generate social models applicable not only in future new towns but also for existing localities. If planned communities are able to provide a more consistently adaptive quality of life, those advantages should be applicable to existing cities.

What are the advantages of the Family Life Center model? First, as already mentioned, the model provides an opportunity for the human services professional to contribute talents to the community outside of the commercial sector, regardless of the nature of his or her paid employment. Thriving communities seldom restrict the exchange of resources and services to the commercial sector. This model has afforded opportunities for community members trained in the behavioral sciences to contribute their talents over a wider range of skills than is sometimes possible through positions of primary employment. Second, the model makes it easier for the community to define the mental health services it desires to have available. Since the Center has no salaried counselors on its staff, it is better able to recruit service deliverers according to the needs expressed by clients. This inductive model of program planning increases the relevance of agency services in relation to the needs of the community. The pool of professional counselors grows according to the needs being expressed by clients of the agency.

The efficacy of its structure for other geographical areas will be tested as the Family Life Center disseminates information nationally to those who seek an efficient economic mental health delivery system. The means for sharing its approach comes from the Family Life Center's major funder: endowments.

While the Family Life Center model is not seen as a replacement for existing models of health services delivery, it may enrich the service capabilities of agencies operating according to other models. Such agencies may expand their roles by relying more on the self-help strengths of the community, thereby taking a significant step toward a pattern of service delivery where human resources are distributed in a more responsive, efficient, and available manner.

11. Developing a Support Base for Women

LOUISE YOLTON EBERHARDT

INTRODUCTION

I have everything in the world to make me happy
—a wonderful husband, two great children, a new
home in a nice community. Why aren't I happy? I
must be the only one in the world who would be so
ungrateful as to feel trapped in a new house, so un-
motherly as to be bored with a new baby, and so
self-centered as to feel unfulfilled in homemaking.

I was raised to get married and have children. That
was my goal. But now the kids are growing up and
I find myself feeling useless and very sad. What can
I do now?

For many women, moving to Columbia meant new
hopes and promises for fulfillment and community which
seemed the answer to many of their problems. However
they found that the new town sometimes referred to as
"the next America" was ill-equipped to provide a new
life-style for women. To be sure there were day-care centers, new homes that were easy to take care of, a wide
variety of recreational facilities and organizations, plus
neighborhood schools and activities for children. The fa-

cilities and traditional opportunities (i.e., garden clubs) were available, but the frustrations many women brought with them remained and for some increased. Although no new alternatives had been planned for, a Women's Center developed out of the felt needs of some women living in the new town.

As I worked in the new community in my job as urban associate for the Columbia Cooperative Ministry, I began to meet a number of women who were under great personal stress. They described themselves as unhappy, lonely, and suffering from depression. Most had some college education and some had had careers before marriage or having children. These were women who had reached the goals of society; namely husband, children, and home only to find disillusionment. No one had prepared them for being at home all day with only children for companionship, for the drudgery of housework that is to be done while husbands are away from home sometimes for days and nights at a time.

These women in Columbia were left with the feeling that there must be more to life than what they were experiencing. Probably the most pervasive feeling all the women shared was a lack of confidence and underestimation of their abilities. At home they received little or no feedback concerning their own real abilities and lacked external criteria for evaluating themselves. Many reported defining their lives almost exclusively in terms of the men in their lives. They saw themselves as failures and inadequate as women.

They did not think that other women were experiencing the same feelings and so felt very alone and different. Many women I talked to reported knowing few other women and being dissatisfied with the exclusively home-centered conversations they shared with the women they did get to know, which only compounded their feelings of isolation. I discovered that they did not have any forums and did not easily talk with one another about personal problems centering around identity. Thus they were left alone to struggle with their feelings and they despaired at that isolation.

A SURVEY OF WOMEN'S NEEDS

It's so lonely moving to a new community—I feel far away from my friends and family. I would like to make new friends, but frankly, I don't know where to start.

My education seems so far away. I feel like my mind is going mushy with no one to talk to all day. To give you an idea, it's exciting to go to the market! I wish I had some intellectual stimulation, some means of learning about exciting and interesting things.

In 1974, from a study made of women in Columbia, it was discovered that their needs and interests were not being satisfied by traditional roles. The survey found that the educational level of women in Columbia is substantially higher than that of the rest of the nation's female population; 46 percent of women in the sample had a college degree or had gone beyond college with professional or graduate work compared to only 7 percent of the U.S. female population in general. Sixty-five percent of the women interviewed expressed interest in obtaining further education. Regarding employment, 66 percent of the women in the survey were employed at "Professional or technical jobs" compared to 16 percent of employed women in the general population. Seventy-one percent of Columbia women have children at home. When asked about nursery and day-care facilities in the new town, existing programs were supported by no less than 73 percent. Only 10 percent wanted to spend more time in homemaking activities and 37 percent prefer to spend less time cleaning, cooking, shopping, or doing similar tasks.

Conclusions and recommendations drawn from this survey established women's needs in Columbia for specific mental health programs and marital counseling, for career counseling and help in sorting through their interests, goals, and values. It also concluded that because so many women feel uprooted and lonely during the first six months in a new community, programs which aid the adjustment process by facilitating friendships and involvement in the community are important.

THE DEVELOPMENT OF THE WOMEN'S CENTER

As part of my work, I began to meet with a small group of women in homes once a week to talk about what was happening in their lives. This group began in 1969 and lasted for a year and a half with some women leaving and new women coming into the group.

What is now known as the Women's Center grew from this series of weekly discussions and from some women in the congregations of the Columbia Cooperative Ministry who felt Columbia should be offering a program for women other than the traditional women's organizations. More women were turned on to the idea and after meeting together for a month, we came up with the concept of "It's Open for Women," offering two weekly programs in a coffee house: one, a speaker presentation; the other, an experiential education program, both providing child care while the woman was away from home. The Columbia Cooperative Ministry subsidized both meeting and child care space plus my time to work with the women in developing this program. For women feeling depressed, lonely, and frustrated, here was a place to get together and talk about their feelings, a place with a supportive atmosphere for self-discovery and stimulation.

From this very modest beginning in 1970, the Women's Center now has an organizational structure, a larger meeting place, a salaried director, and close to 100 dedicated volunteers who manage all of the program activities. As word has gotten around, new discussion groups and services have developed out of the needs new women bring to the center. More than 2,000 women have participated in center activities and an average of 200 attend weekly programming.

The structure and programming of the Women's Center lends itself to participation on many different levels. Some may only attend a lecture once or twice a year, while many others attend weekly or biweekly sessions. The women who come are not pressured to go in any direction or at any speed. For many it is the first time they have experienced genuine care and support from other women. It is a place where deep friendships develop between women.

The center is open four to five mornings per week. Large group lectures are presented on Tuesday mornings, discussion groups on Wednesdays, experiential education sessions on Thursdays, and small groups convene periodically. The center publishes a monthly journal which reaches over 300 women in its mail circulation alone. The center also operates a child care center where preschoolers of any age may be left under professional care in the same building while mothers attend programs or meetings. No other day-care facility in Columbia offers child care for children under the age of two.

WHO ATTENDS THE CENTER

In a survey conducted last year of the women who attended the center, it was revealed that 91 percent of the women are currently married and have children. Although the children of the women in this sample ranged from infants to young adults, 59 percent of the children were preschool and under two years of age. The age range of the women in the survey was from 20 to 50 with 69 percent of this group between 26 and 35 years. More than

50 percent of the women had worked in the past or volunteered on a part-time basis. Of statistical and sociological significance was the fact that 70 percent of the respondents were not affiliated with any other groups that related to women in or outside Columbia. Thus one can see that the women who come to the center are not women who are active in the community or work full time. Most are married, are mothers with small children and have little involvement in activities outside the home.

GOALS AND PHILOSOPHY

The primary goals of the center are to reach, encourage, and provide the means for women to experience themselves as complete human beings and unique individuals with power over their own lives and the ability to influence their total communities.

It is the philosophy of the center that women learn to lead their own programs, and training of such women has been included in all aspects of the center. The focus in many other institutions has been that some one else has the problem. At the Women's Center we believe in helping each other to help ourselves. The focus of the programs is not problem solving as much as it is sharing or learning new skills. The women leaders are there to help provide the atmosphere, help the groups reach deeper levels of sharing, help each woman make her own decisions, and share themselves. Advice is not encouraged to prevent any woman from becoming an authority figure.

A group of volunteers who have received and continue to receive training in experiential education, design programs to develop human relations skills. Inservice programs, outside consultants, and training organizations such as the Mid-Atlantic Training Committee in Washington, D.C. are all used to train the women, with the emphasis on inservice training. They are all women who have evidenced interest and/or potential ability through their participation in the Women's Center programs. As the women see themselves as effective and competent persons they want to give and contribute to the other women in the Center in this way. At this point they have gotten what they need from participating in the programs and want to further grow by learning leadership and facilitating skills.

Even though we do have defined leaders, we operate on a sharing model and women experience women as helping each other and feel a combined power and energy. At the Center women become aware of the competitive and conditioned attitudes they often have had toward other women and try out new behavior based on cooperation and sharing. This noncompetitive environment is one one of the most unique features of the Center, where women can grow without the fear of failure and where they can share their skills.

Women move out of the Center after a year or two and move into new jobs, return to school, and attain leadership positions in the community. For example, two women who were active for several years in the Center first as participants and then as leaders have successfully started their own business. They credit their ability and confidence to risk such a venture to their experience at the Women's Center. Another woman who felt she had little to offer when coming to the Center as a participant gained confidence and became part of the leadership team. She then went on to finish her masters thesis in psychology and is now in the counseling department at a large university. Other have left the Center to go to law school, return to old careers, and to develop new community services and organizations.

This shifting leadership every year or two makes for a less rigid core of leaders and gives others an opportunity to develop leadership skills. It also means the flavor of the Center does change to some extent depending on who is active that year in leading the programs. We believe this to be a healthy model.

PROGRAMS

The Center's programs are different from the traditional social work and psychiatric institution for much of
the emphasis is sociological. That is, a woman's problems
or feelings are not just dealt with individually but are seen
in terms of the socialization process all women receive in
this culture, including the stereotyping and pressures (often very subtle and unconscious) which inhibit women
from using or even developing their potentials and talents. The female experience is validated with other
women and some of the guilt and the feeling of being
alone with one's problems begin to disappear. Yet it is also
stressed that it is important for the individual woman to
start to take responsibility for herself and her actions. She
is encouraged to become a whole person, defined and
validated by herself with the support of other women.

The programs of the Center have emerged out of the
group experience and the various needs that the women
express. Programs sometime last for a short period of
time; other programs have been important throughout
the life of the Center and they are described in the following paragraphs.

Issue Forums

Involving speakers and panel presentations, issue
forums provide for the exchange of information and opin-
ions on a wide range of topics. This large group forum
(often more than 100 participants) tends to arouse the
woman's interests in a wider range of activities that not
only contribute to her self-awareness and outlook on life,
but also contribute to her participation in community activities and services. Certain topics generate particular
excitement and new spin-offs or new community groups
have been started as a result, e.g., Howard County Woman's Political Caucus. In essence, the real aim of this

program is to begin to break down the barriers that have produced social isolation for so many of the women.

The Experiential Education

This program is organized as an introduction to the examination of self, including goals, values, life-styles, and interpersonal communication. Each week an experience is designed by a team of skilled leaders. Each planned activity is designed with a specific learning objective and the sequence of activities is ordered to move in the direction of anticipated outcomes or goals. After participating in the experience, the women with the help of the facilitators reflect on what happened, how they felt about it, and what they learned. Most women who participate (30 approximately) want to change or grow in some way.

> Through the simulated games, exercises and role plays, I've had a chance to look at myself in relation to my husband and family, to work on such things as communication skills, and to think about some personal goals which will allow me to use my talents and abilities. I like the structure of the Thursday programs: It's a place where I know someone is setting it up for me to discover something about myself.

Discussion Group

This program is offered by a team of leaders for women to share with other women their experiences and views about topics that concern them such as marriage, body image, and money and its impact on relationships. Here is a time when women discover they are not alone in many of their concerns, problems, emotions, and fears. It is also an opportunity to begin to discover alternative ways of dealing with such concerns.

As a regular participant at the Wednesday programs, I have had the opportunity to make new friendships which I have come to treasure. For me, in a very real sense, this group has taken the place of the extended family. The atmosphere is warm and non-threatening. I've seen that each person who comes possesses different backgrounds and values. But we all try to listen and not impose our values on each other. The discussion group has been my first exposure to a "human" approach to problems. As a direct result of sharing thoughts and feelings on a new, deeper level, I've learned that I really enjoy talking to other women.

Small Group Experiences

The most in-depth programs for women to learn about themselves are the small group experiences which meet once a week for eight weeks. Together with 8 or 10 other women, she is encouraged to examine herself and to try out new behavior while looking at such questions as: Who am I apart from my husband and children? How do I come across to others? Do I want to change and if I do, how? The groups offered include: "In Search of Yourself," "Female Sexuality," "Power and Aggression"; plus groups for specific women such as "Divorce, Separated Group," "35 Plus," and "Black Women."

Agencies such as the Catholic Social Services and the Columbia Mental Health Center often refer clients to our small groups. They feel we are a viable alternative to psychiatric or psychological counseling for women in the community. We are viewed as functioning as a preventive mental health center because many women who come receive help before an emotional or marital crisis occurs.

As women begin to change and grow, it has an impact on the family, particularly the marriage relationship. The Women's Center offers several groups, such as a male/female roles groups and marriage enrichment weekends, to help deal with the conflicts and issues. It is also interest-

ing to note that several men's support groups have started
after their wives started participating in the center.

How the Center Operates

The Center functions with an operating budget of
$10,000. The Columbia Cooperative Ministry has pro-
vided space (three to four rooms for each program) and
the part-time salary of the coordinator. Other than the
church, which is withdrawing funds in the near future, no
other institution has been willing to support the Center
financially.

A small admission charge and nominal child care fee is
collected at each program if a woman can pay. These fees
and fund raising events pay the maintenance costs of the
Center. Space is a problem in a new town where there are
no "cheap" old buildings to be had and thus organizations
such as ours must rely on donated space and renegotiate
every year for such space.

There are 50 to 70 volunteer staff who give 5 to 15 hours
a week to the Center. In addition to administrative tasks,
the coordinator is expected to carry out such functions as
inservice training, public relations, developing new programs, and fund raising. There is a need for additional
paid staff to carry out some of these functions more adequately.

Afterthoughts

If I were starting again I would be more of an advocate
with the developer and other institutions, encouraging
them to be more responsive to the needs of women moving into a new town. The developers could hire a consultant on women's needs who could help organizations like
the Women's Center begin and find adequate funding
(which has taken up so much time and energy for so little

return). It might also have been helpful to have a support group of persons in the community who represent other organizations and constituencies whose function would be to represent us in the community and help us with funding.

Summary

The Women's Center programs are a time for a woman to be with herself, to begin to get her needs met, to discover more of herself. Some come at first in hopes of meeting a friend, to have time away from children, out of curiosity or boredom, or in search of a new direction in their life. They find the Center to be a source of external support offering both companionship, understanding and caring; replacing the traditional supports of an extended family and close friends. For many women this is their first exchange of frank and honest communication with other women. In sharing confidences, they find that women are likeable, intelligent, and important persons; in turn they begin to believe they are also.

The Center has provided the often needed channel for many women to bridge the gap from years of child rearing or homemaking to reentry into community activities, the business world, or the academic community. It has provided support and direction to women at points of transition in their lives, such as becoming parents, undergoing separation or divorce, or other personal crises. And most importantly the Center has been an environment for women to appreciate their own potentials and abilities, to discover new ways of relating to others and to learn new skills. Many feel that the Women's Center has changed their lives. It should be a good model for other communities.

12. Black Involvement in a New Community

JEAN WARRICK TOOMER

Many American words and phrases, especially those related to quality of life, hold different meanings for different people and, because of the realities in American life, thus arouse different expectations, "Freedom," "integration," "pursuit of happiness," "all men are created equal," and "liberty and justice for all" historically have held one set of expectations and realities for the Founding Fathers and those able to make it in our society and quite another for those who have had to struggle for survival and fight for opportunities to realize their goals and aspirations.

Columbia, Maryland, the planned community billed as the Next America, is different in many ways from the America that most of us know. In it we have open housing, open enrollment in schools, and open access to all commercial and noncommercial facilities and institutions. However, people moved here with differing expectations, sometimes tied to national rhetoric and sometimes tied to rhetoric specific to Columbia, such as "quality of life," "human potential and growth," "caring community," "citizen involvement," and the term "Next America" itself.

Though not a trained behavioral scientist, I have agreed to contribute my thoughts to this publication because I know that many city planners have taken Columbia as a model and many others are expected to do the same. They will presumably duplicate the excellent physical planning which has made Columbia one of the most physically attractive communities I have seen and will be influenced by the social concept, which also holds great potential. I fear, however, that planners will also duplicate serious flaws and omissions in Columbia's social planning. This article discusses certain flaws and omissions as I have observed and experienced them.

PERSONAL HISTORY AND PERSPECTIVE

I write from the perspective of a black middle-class resident who has lived in Columbia for seven and a half years with my husband and five children ranging in age from fifteen to four when we moved here. I have been active both as a community volunteer and as a paid employee in the area of community services. Educated in black institutions which stressed Negro history and pride in our race, I also grew up in a generation which emulated white middle-class life styles and had integration as its goal. This paradox was not as frustrating as it might appear because the emphasis on racial pride also carried with it the absolute conviction that blacks were as intelligent, skillful, talented, and equal in potential as any other race, given equal opportunities. In addition to open housing, open school enrollment, and the freedom to spend money in any establishment, integration also meant a significant share in the power and decision-making processes affecting everyday life. With the progress of the civil rights struggle over the years, I and many others of my generation thought that when we reached the high point of the movement in the 1960's the opportunity for blacks to reach their full potential in American society had finally arrived. After seeing advertisements on Columbia, the Next America, I was sure of it.

I have often commented on the naiveté which many people, both black and white, have had about Columbia. When we moved in, I had, for example, naively equated the developer's commitment to open housing with my definition of integration. Though I never sat down and listed my expectations for living in this new community, in retrospect I realize they were there. I also now realize the part that rhetoric about the Next America played in raising my expectations. I expected more from Columbia than from other communities. Thus, I might have been pleasantly surprised to find blacks in decision-making positions in other suburban communities, whereas I expected them to occupy such positions in Columbia and was especially disappointed to find none. For the purpose of this paper I have designated these phenomena as "expectations."

I am deeply grateful to our children, especially the older ones, and my friends in this community—black and white, young and old—who have helped raise my level of racial consciousness and my recognition of the need for it in others. However, it should be understood that this paper reflects my personal views and may or may not reflect others' perceptions.

I have categorized my thoughts into three main areas: (1) my expectations of Columbia; (2) my reality of living in the community; and (3) my views on the potential for black involvement in planning and developing a new town. These areas are applied to certain aspects of life with which I am most familiar: the school system, social services, and black involvement in life in general.

THE SCHOOL SYSTEM

Expectations

I arrived in Columbia knowing that the schools were under the County's educational district and that for the

first few years there would be no middle or high school in
Columbia for our two teenagers. I knew that Columbia's
schools were to follow an open space concept, which
meant both large open areas architecturally and an innovative approach instructionally. Thus, I was spared the
frustrations of some parents who were not aware that
their older children's school locations were outside of Columbia, of others who had not thought through the risks
of having their children be part of a completely different
approach to education than they or their children had
been used to, or of still others who believed there was a
distinct "Columbia School System."

I did, however, have other expectations which were not
fully realized. Because I had had excellent black teachers
and administrators in my own educational experience up
to and including graduate school, and because I knew
there have always been competent blacks in these areas,
I had expected to find blacks more involved as part of the
school structure. I knew the developer had no control
over the school system as a whole; nevertheless, it was still
an expectation for me in the Next America.

Reality

Columbians have access to open enrollment in Howard
County schools in two ways: first, there is open housing as
well as economic diversity of housing in Columbia's several neighborhoods and the school districts are based on
neighborhoods; second, Howard County allows a choice
of schools so long as a facility is not overcrowded and
parents provide transportation as needed. As a result Columbia's student population has always been integrated.
However, there was not when we arrived nor is there now
a sufficient number of blacks in the administrative and
decision-making structure to make an impact on the system from within.

Both as a concerned parent and a member of a school
Human Relations Committee, I became aware of con-

scious and even more harmful unconscious racism that permeated several schools and the system in general. Fortunately, improvements are being made. There has been an increase in the number of black teachers and principals and community efforts have led to the appointment of a Human Relations Specialist on the Superintendent's staff. The Howard County chapter of the NAACP continues to monitor and report policies adversely affecting black students and teachers. One such study, for example, concerned the disproportionate suspension of black pupils. There is still much to be done.

Potential

There are areas of life in new towns over which developers have little or no control. Very often the school system is such an area. In Columbia, because the developer was willing to donate land for all schools to be built here and because the county was already in the process of establishing a model open space school system, there was a cooperative atmosphere between the school board and the developer and many of the latter's ideas on architecture and land use were accepted.

A developer has the additional potential for trying to raise the awareness of school officials regarding racial tensions and how to deal with them. To do so, however, both developers and planners themselves must reach a certain level of awareness. The same kind of concern given to land use, design, and such possibilities as community use of schools can and should be directed towards creating mechanisms for dealing with the 200 years of racism that remains prevalent in attitudes, textbooks, curricula, and administrative policies, not to mention the human racial tensions that result in the schools themselves. If a school system is not amenable to such input, then it is incumbent on the developer to express this concern outside the school system through development of separate mechanisms. The problem is difficult but that is not to say that solutions should not be attempted. I believe that if enough blacks were involved in the planning process, the problem itself will not simply be overlooked or avoided.

SOCIAL SERVICES

Expectations

I had no personal expectations of using social services because our family had never needed such resources. I only became aware of many people's expectations and needs as I began to work in the community service area as coordinator of volunteers for the Columbia Association. My staff and I received many requests for assistance or information from blacks and whites, handicapped and disabled, and young and old with reference to county services, counseling for individuals and families, emergency help of money or services, and ways to deal with the trauma of moving to a new town or with the tensions (usually racial) of coming in contact with Columbia's diversity. I did develop a personal need for after school care for my children when I began to work full time.

Reality

Here again words have meant different things to different people. When one hears about social planning in Columbia, it is usually in relation to cul-de-sacs, cluster mailboxes, or the economic housing mix. Columbia also has been committed to early childhood education, represented by a variety of nonprofit and proprietary day care and nursery school programs, and to programs for teenagers. In fact, many different approaches and much money and time have been invested in dealing with the "teen problem." Unfortunately, solutions still seem very far away and will continue to remain so until the adult community and power structure are prepared to deal with racial concerns.

In addition to the provision of facilities and specialized programs, social planning also includes ways to deal with problems which arise when people of varying backgrounds live in proximity to each other as well as ways to make facilities and programs physically, financially, and culturally accessible to everyone. In conversations with some persons involved in planning Columbia I have concluded that certain basic assumptions were made: first, social service meant social welfare (and there was very little indication there would be many Columbians on welfare); second, social problems are not the responsibility of the developer and, therefore, programs for dealing with such problems are not his responsibility; third, even if such problems and programs were the developer's responsibility, the timing of planning new towns is such that problems, and thus their solutions, would change materially between the time of planning and the time residents would be moving in (examples often cited are, "Who involved in planning Columbia during the early 1960's could have predicted subsequent youth and black revolutions which swept the nation?"); and fourth, residents of a community are the only ones who can identify the social problems confronting them, set priorities, and determine solutions. So it must be left to residents after the community has taken shape to deal with this entire area of concern.

Potential

My ideas on social service potentials in new communities take issue with the above viewpoints. First, social service does not mean social welfare and the various social service institutions that have emerged in Columbia attest to that fact. Various counseling services, the youth employment service, a before and after school child care program are all examples. Second, the same mentality that allows a developer to believe that planners having expertise in land use, architecture, and the development of recreational, religious, and medical facilities can design a community which will be better than urban sprawl could (and should) believe that it is equally important to utilize expertise and planning concerning human problems in order to prevent and alleviate stress in these areas. Third, while it is true one cannot precisely predict problems or ways to deal with them, developers can be safe in predicting that there will be human concerns and can, therefore, establish mechanisms for facilitating the search for solutions. Fourth, it is no more reasonable to expect citizens of new towns to develop and operate institutions for meeting human needs without wholehearted staff support than it is to expect them singlehandedly to maintain the physical appearance of public land and buildings, recreational and other physical facilities.

Dealing with human concerns is always more difficult, entails more risk, and needs far more than monetary commitment. Developers and planners have an opportunity both to set a tone of empathy and caring and to provide mechanisms and resources whereby human needs receive at least as much professional attention as physical ones.

GENERAL BLACK INVOLVEMENT

Expectations

While I expected that I would be living in a predominantly white world in Columbia, I believed there would be significant black involvement in its power structure. I had not given it a lot of thought but I did expect to be employed in the community after our younger children were in school. I was excited and challenged about working in a community that really cared about people.

Reality

I first became aware there was no significant black involvement in the systematic structure of the Next America by the absence of blacks from staffs of the land sales office, builders, realtors, and any of the usual contacts one makes in negotiating for a home. There were few blacks in any visible skilled jobs on the numerous buildings in progress at that time, although a black builder was involved in Columbia for a brief period. Now, in addition to black-owned real estate firms, there are many black real estate salespeople in the community and blacks are involved in some of the building firms.

When I became more deeply involved as a resident and employee, I became more aware that in the power structure over which the developer had no apparent control there were no blacks in positions of authority. In fact, the school administration, including the community college, county government, voluntary agencies, medical facility, and newspapers not only were controlled by whites but in many instances had no black staff members. When there was one, there was *only* one. Those of us who have been in that position know what an impossible struggle is involved in such tokenism. Some improvements have been made but blacks still are not involved significantly in many of these areas.

In areas over which the developer does have control, such as the Executive Committee of the Columbia Association (the organization set up to manage Columbia's facilities and to which every resident pays an assessment) and the staff of the Howard Research and Development Corporation (the firm which is developing Columbia), there were few blacks in positions of authority. After eight years there has still not been a black appointed by the developer to the Executive Committee of the Columbia Association and there has not been a black in the Association's top management.

Columbia's governance system allows for open political

involvement of residents in advisory capacities and, depending on the number of occupied housing units in a village, a voting position on the Columbia Association's Executive Committee. In the early days, just as the formal system did not include blacks, few blacks involved themselves in the informal open political process. This is perhaps understandable. After the struggle in the other America to find a decent place to live without a cross burning on the lawn, to have schools that black children could attend without a sense of fear and concern for their safety, and to be able to go and come at will in any of the areas of community life, blacks could be expected to wish to relax and enjoy, at least for awhile. Now, however, there are many blacks involved in the political process and several black organizations have been formed. There are more black people in Columbia than in the early days and they are much more aware than before of the need to become involved in improving the community in general and providing black input, in particular.

Potential

The potential for black involvement in new towns is limitless. In this age of blacks with expertise in planning, engineering, economics, social science, community development, behavioral science, and any other professional area, the old argument of "no qualified blacks" simply does not hold. An essential ingredient for meaningful black involvement is a commitment to find and, most important, to listen to black input even when (especially when) that input reflects viewpoints differing from those of the white majority. It is also important to have several blacks, not just one, involved in the various processes through which policy and action decisions are made. Blacks, no matter how diverse in experience, education, life style, and values, have the commonality of having been dehumanized, rejected, and made to feel invisible in numerous ways in this country. Two or more blacks working in the same setting support one another in drawing from their commonality of experience to express an empathy for others in similar circumstances. Such input, made seriously and consistently, may not solve all problems in this area, nevertheless, it will represent a giant step towards solutions.

Involvement of varied types of input is essential to good social planning. Blacks are not the only ones to be involved. Handicapped people also must have input when facilities are planned to serve an entire community. Senior citizens, young people, and other groups with special needs also must have the opportunity to participate. When planning *inclusive* communities, care must be taken to ensure that they do not become exclusive of certain groups simply because their inputs were lacking.

In new towns as well as elsewhere, the struggle for racial equality is not over. The system must continue to be pressed for black inclusion in the decision-making processes of new communities just as in old ones. Blacks, too, share a responsibility for involving themselves voluntarily. They cannot afford to allow complacency to overtake them as more blacks are included within the formal system for it is important for such progress to be supported and maintained on all fronts. Many middle-class black Columbians are involved in the voluntary sector and many more are becoming aware of the need to do so. The enormity of the struggle for equality lies ahead for several generations. There continue to be enough instances which have proved that "until all of us have made it, none of us has," and we have to be our brothers' keeper. The black middle class risks becoming prisoners in expensive homes just as the white middle class. Both blacks and whites must show concern and take steps to improve the quality of life for everyone as brothers, not only because of idealistic motives but also for their own survival.

CONCLUSION

The purpose of this contribution has not been to detract from how far we have come as a nation or as a planned new community in moving towards the goals embodied both in the national and Columbia rhetoric referred to earlier. Instead, the purpose has been to point out how empty that rhetoric becomes when the words and phrases do not apply to all who hear them, for each person has the right to expect that the rhetoric applies to oneself. This paper has been written in the spirit that it is desirable to subject such rhetoric to continuous measurement and evaluation and, when necessary, to press for corrective action if our national purpose is ever to be achieved.

13.   Teenagers in Columbia[1]

ROGER KARSK
DONALD C. KLEIN

Physical realities of Columbia dictate a great deal about teenager activities and their locations in this new town. There is no concentrated downtown such as depicted in the recent movie *American Graffiti*. There are no drive-in restaurants, a teenage institution of the 1950's and 1960's. For those who grew up in the city there are literally no street corners on which to "hang out." Many restaurants were planned for the new community, but only two to date have catered to teenagers (and they no longer exist). In fact, most discourage teenagers from coming into their establishments unless they are going to buy something besides a coke. The very physical plan dictates where teenagers will *not* go simply because many of the traditional locations for teenagers are not available. On the other hand, there are amenities offered in Columbia for teenagers that most other communities of comparable size do not have. Each of Columbia's first three village

---

[1]The majority of the data for this article came from a two-year NIMH research grant through the Center for Metropolitan Problems and administered through CoRAL,II. Data were gathered from March 1972–September 1974. Teenagers for the study were 15 or older.

123

centers had space set aside for teenagers: there are ten swimming pools, an ice skating rink, numerous tennis courts, many parks, three lakes, a comprehensive recreation program, and a range of programs in art, music, drama, and dance.

Most Columbia teenagers come from families earning substantial incomes, generally in excess of $20,000. In many of their families both parents work, and most live in detached homes, even though Columbia has a diverse housing distribution including townhouses and apartments. There is a feeling of far more teenagers on the street than the population's statistics indicate. Only 7 percent of the population is between 13 and 18. A larger percentage (15 percent) is moving into the teenage years. Although Columbia's population has tended to be quite mobile prior to moving here, almost half of the teenagers have lived in the city over three years and only 16 percent less than one year. Although 16 percent of the overall population is black, some 23 percent of the teenagers are black.

In general, teenagers have a positive view of Columbia. In a survey of 100 teenagers and their parents, 66 percent of the teenagers said they like living in Columbia with only 7 percent disagreeing. Over 70 percent of the parents interviewed felt that teens liked living in Columbia. Some reasons given for liking Columbia were its friendliness, safety, there were more friends, and there was more to do.

As part of the study eight teens, all 15 or older, from different socioeconomic backgrounds and locations of residence were hired to keep a detailed log of their activities over a one-year period of time. The work experience of the log keepers pointed to another positive resource for teenagers: the possibility of obtaining jobs. There were ample opportunities due to: (1) availability of jobs within the many retail shops at the village centers and the Mall, and at various construction sites; (2) adults not taking service jobs due to their high level of education (the teens are

sought to fill such jobs as sales clerks, maintenance workers, and waitresses); and (3) the nonprofit Youth Employment Service, sponsored originally by the Columbia
Association, which among other services provides teens
under 16 with part-time jobs and maintains a referral
service for full-time employment.

For those interested in on-going athletics and structured programs, Columbia is an enormously rich community. There are excellent opportunities to participate in
sports and a large option of other programs ranging from
karate to aircraft flying. The Columbia Association model
also provides an on-going mechanism to assure that funds
are available for future allocation. During one recent
year, over $120,000 was designated for the teenage area.

Inquiring into teenagers' interactions with their peers
we found that the log keepers had an average of five close
friends apiece. Those friends tended to be very much like
the log keepers in terms of family income, race, type of
housing, location of residence, and attending the same
high school. There was very little crossing of either racial
or socioeconomic lines.

Attempting to answer the question of what teenagers
do in Columbia, we found that private homes were used
as the most common place for activities such as meeting
friends, private parties, or watching television. The most
common public facility used by all teenagers was the
downtown covered shopping Mall. They went there on
the average of one time per week; some went just to
"hang out" and meet their friends, although several went
because of a job or to buy something. The recreational
amenities of the community were used very sparingly by
the teens we followed. They went swimming during the
summer, for instance, less than once every two weeks.
The lake area in downtown Columbia was an attraction
for many teenagers during the summer; our log keepers
went there on the average of one time per week.

There has been much controversy over the viability of
teenager centers. Part of the controversy stemmed from

the lack of clear-cut goals for a successful teenage center. Was it successful if a certain percentage of them used it, or was it successful if only a few used it but were diverted from deviant behavior? Our survey showed that only 20 percent said they had been to a center at least once, whereas 43 percent thought *other* teenagers went there. Only one of the log keepers went to the centers with any regularity.

Each one of Columbia's centers went through very much the same history. They started out with a primarily white, middle-class clientele in their early teens, usually coming from the village where the center was located. The same ones would continue to go to the center until they were 15 or 16. At this point the center would be approximately two years old. Black teenagers, generally from the rent supplement housing or from rural Howard County, then began to infiltrate the center. White teenagers felt hassled by blacks enough to make them not want to come back. Blacks would then declare the center "their turf," and most whites avoided the center and the area immediately around it.

Reviewing the original plans, we found that a great many ideas had been generated but that no firm directions had been set. Self-contained teenage centers were not highly favored in those early documents. Recommendations were made that space be made available in multipurpose community facilities if teenagers requested it but not labelled as teenage centers. In the actual implementations, however, the centers came into existence more by happenstance than by careful design.

In Columbia emphasis has been put on physical planning and facilities as the means to meeting teenagers' needs. Our study shows that they do use these facilities but not nearly to the extent that was anticipated. Support also has been given to traditional recreational programs such as soccer, swimming, basketball leagues and a variety of short courses. By contrast, little has been made available in regard to helping teenagers through the psychosocial transition of adolescence. Two examples are issues with parents and issues relating to class and race.

In the area of family, many of the teenagers we talked with were wrestling with problems concerning "separation" from one's parents. How could they begin to lead lives that were not totally dependent on their parents? Although there are crisis resources in Columbia, such as Grassroots,[2] there are no identified resources the teenagers can turn to just to talk, such as an outreach or social worker.

The ones who moved into the 600 rent supplement housing units tended to bring a different value system with them from those living in other parts of Columbia. They tend to be black and from the inner city (whites living in the units are younger with preschool children or are over 65). These black teenagers are much more used to overt conflict than either their black or white middle-class counterparts. Many of them have never associated with whites and vice versa, leading to a mistrust of each other. Much of the conflict was written up in the local papers as being racial in nature, and it was partly, but there are also economic and class differences involved. Few of the middle-class black teenagers were part of the harassments. There were no programs or people to assist the transition or to help each group understand the other. It was generally left to the high schools to provide whatever leadership there was to work on racial and socioeconomic tensions.

Single solutions have been used repeatedly. When these solutions have not worked the adult community has become exasperated. Teenagers have tended to be treated like a group with a problem that can be solved rather than recognizing that teens, like other groups, require a variety of different resources.

Despite the deficiencies, Columbia seems to be a positive place for adolescents to grow up. There are possibili-

[2]Described elsewhere in this monograph.

ties here for jobs and better recreational facilities and programs than in most other communities; they see the community as basically friendly and a good place to be.

Given our findings for Columbia there are some things that can be suggested for meeting the needs of teenagers and for a better understanding between adolescents and the adult community in Columbia and other localities:

—Physical facilities are important but emphasis needs to go beyond physical solutions and include careful attention to human resources. Teenagers who are not interested in formal programs might be reached through outreach workers.

—There needs to be an acknowledgment of the special identity concerns of certain black teenagers from lower socioeconomic income levels. There seems to be a much greater need among this group to control physical space than among the middle-class either white or black.

—There needs to be some meaningful way to involve teenagers more vitally in the life of the community including its governance. Part of the frustration on the part of Columbia's governance is trying to determine who represents them.

—Although there is a physical map outlining the future of Columbia, there is no such "map" for dealing with the growing teenage population. Such a planning process would put any locality in the desirable position of being proactive in the teenage area rather than reactive as Columbia has tended to be in the past.

—Rather than looking for the one ideal program that would solve all the problems there should be some on-going support of institutions that have already been identified by teenagers as valuable resources. Two such institutions in Columbia are Grassroots and the Youth Employment Service.

—It is important that there be some on-going monitoring system because there is a rapid turnover of generations in the teen area. Coupled with this is the realization that solving a problem with today's teenagers does not necessarily mean it will stay solved. There are both new teenagers moving into adolescence and more are moving into the Columbia community as it grows to maturity.

From our admittedly biased viewpoint, Columbia has the ingredients of being a good place for teenagers to live, learn, work, play and set their future directions. It has a diverse population, job opportunities, economic resources that can be put into the teenage area, and a flexible governance that can respond to needs. Columbia is a good place for teenagers, with the potential to be better. Our impression is that the process of experimentation and redesign is well under way and will continue. Columbia has the potential for turning its teenage problems into opportunities.

Section III

THE COMMUNITY PSYCHOLOGIST AS CITIZEN-PRACTITIONER IN NEW COMMUNITY SETTINGS

14. Introduction

Section III consists of two papers that provide first person accounts of the activities of psychologists who sought to make their psychological skills and knowledge relevant to the process of community building in Columbia and elsewhere. It complements previous articles in the monograph that have touched on the work of community psychologists in new towns: having to do with application of psychological knowledge to community design (Murrell); with research intended to shape policy and planning (Karsk and Klein); with conceptualizing the processes whereby new institutions can be helped to emerge (Wastie and Klein); with the creation of self-help counseling and support services (Feinstein); with the development and management of innovative organizational forms (Shoffeit & Shoffeit).

The contribution by husband-wife pair Carlotta and Carl Young is concerned with how community psychology skills were translated into neighboring activities on the part of a young family in an enclave of town houses. The Youngs make little distinction between the work of a community psychologist as a professional person and the community psychology of professional-citizens within their own neighborhoods. The paper is an account of what happened when they set out to help develop a sense of community in their immediate environs.

In her contribution Doris Wright describes the transformation of a counseling psychologist into a social engineer of community design. Wright steeped herself in the problems and approaches of planners and developers both in Columbia and a corollary project carried out in Hartford, Connecticut. Her work has involved her in a wide range of projects largely unexplored by most community psychologists.

I hope what will stand out for the reader in this section —as well as in the previous sections' accounts of social scientists' work in new towns—is the sense of challenge and excitement which can be generated when community psychologists find ways to become involved in the design and implementation of planned environments for large numbers of people.

15. *Community Psychology on a Cul-de-Sac*

CARLOTTA J. YOUNG
CARL E. YOUNG

Our professional and private lives have been inter-twined in Columbia. We have been committed to "making Columbia work," that is, to its becoming a model community in the minds of its residents. Thus, we have tried to use our psychological education and training in our various community activities, especially those involving the 40 townhouses on our cul-de-sac (a dead-end street, usually no more than a block in length). In this paper we shall describe briefly 1) why we value community development at the small neighborhood or street level; 2) the physical design of housing on our cul-de-sac; 3) some characteristics of its residents; and 4) our own role in and appraisal of some specific community activities that we think would be of interest to community psychologists and others.

Like many of our neighbors, we were initially attracted to Columbia because of its amenities, esthetic design, and promise of more intimate, primary group types of associations. The latter was especially important for we have grown up in small towns where activities with neighbors were common. Moreover, we had enjoyed the network of friendships that emerged because of proximity in the

135

housing project and neighborhoods where we lived during graduate school. In Columbia, we envisioned the opportunity of creating friendships not only through our usual mode of reference group associations (e.g., work, professional groups, church) but through our membership in a specific neighborhood as well. Close neighboring ties were valued because they contributed to our feelings of community and security, to repeated casual interactions, to services such as last-minute child care, etc.

Mutual support and social participation are essential community characteristics, and their absence is often cited in criticisms of modern suburbia. Since both play an important role in how people think about themselves and their community, their relative absence or presence may well ultimately determine Columbia's success as a new town. There is ample evidence that neither will necessarily develop naturally among residents who desire it. But fortunately there are ways to encourage their development at the specific neighborhood level. While community development and identification is also important at larger and more complex levels, the neighborhood level offers several advantages: less coordination is needed, task definition is easier, motivation is higher, and the friendship network that results is daily rewarding.

Townhouses (rowhouses), condominiums, and apartments differ from single-family homes in that they have explicit boundaries and higher densities, have common structural characteristics, and promote shared interests. Of these, townhouses such as those on our cul-de-sac (CDS) had private doorsteps or entrances and mini-yards. There were 40 units on our CDS, 12 of which were separated from the others in that they are closer to the entrance and north of the community mail box. Interestingly, the 12 units north of the mail box had formed traditionally a special mini-community of their own and originally had limited interaction with the other 28 units. As a neighbor once put it, "They might as well be in Topeka." The families on the CDS were quite young, usually in their late 20's or early 30's. Only a few families had children in high school. Turnover among the residents was common. The units were completed in 1970; but less than six of the original families remain. Most of the families leaving the CDS move into larger single-family dwelling units elsewhere in Columbia. Only five or six families were renting.

In spite of the rather high turnover, a close sense of community existed among the CDS residents. It is expressed in and enhanced by cooperative efforts that will be briefly summarized below.

COOPERATIVE OWNERSHIP

After buying our townhouse, we were informed that we now owned 25 percent of a lawn mower. (Over ten families now use it.) We liked the idea so much that we began seeking other cooperative ownerships. Our list now includes a long ladder, a power saw, gardening tools, a set of car-tuning instruments, and a volleyball set. The volleyball set, which is set up in the street, has proved very popular. As many as 30 people—men, women, and children—have participated at the same time, with most of the other neighbors freely substituting and cheering.

DIRECTORY

Remembering and using names is a time-honored aid in forming friendships, yet 40 units represent a lot of names. Therefore, we put together and distributed a simple directory of family members' names, children's ages, work information, and special interests (e.g., gardening, weaving, sailing). Listing of any or all information about residents was, of course, completely voluntary. Another family plans a follow-up directory of other voluntary information, including equipment (e.g., tools, ice cream machine, crab steamer) that different persons would be willing to loan as part of a cooperative effort.

INNOVATION DIFFUSION

Since all of the townhouses are structurally identical, good interior designs and other improvements are quickly adapted by others. Thus, new and old residents alike enjoy seeing how others have fixed up their units. As a result, discussion and consultation about design is a common form of social interchange that helps the socialization process, particularly for new residents. Plans are being made to have "open houses" some Sunday afternoon to show off some of the more innovative designs.

BLOCK PARTIES

As mentioned earlier, the families who lived north of the mailbox had very little interaction with those who lived south of it. Several of the neighbors organized an outdoor block party during each of the last two summers and asked each family to bring a covered dish. Nearly everyone participated, and new friendships were formed. As a consequence, the "mailbox parallel" is now largely historical. Parenthetically, the street's community mail center, which includes individual letter and package compartments, a drop box, and stamp dispenser, serves as a casual meeting place for residents.

WOMEN'S GROUPS

For the woman at home in the CDS during the day there is more opportunity to be with her neighbors than there would be on a street of single-family dwellings. She certainly is more likely to see her neighbors than the man or woman who works outside the home all day. Yet the amount of contact with neighbors varies strikingly. It is influenced by several factors:

1. Whether or not there are small children. If so, then the mother is likely to spend time outside playing with the child, and to meet the parents of each child's playmates.
2. Individual circumstance of the woman. This would depend on whether the woman was outgoing and interested in being with other women, what responsibilities and interests she has inside the house, and what volunteer or educational activities she is involved in away from home.
3. Weather. This is probably the most important single factor. This CDS is very outside-oriented. The custom is to visit outside as you do other things or just to gather informally outside and chat. On a warm day, one woman "stoop sitting" will soon be joined by as many as 4 or 6 more, the group changing as women come and go. There are few structured get-togethers such as a morning coffee at someone's house to meet a new neighbor. Thus, to arrive in the fall essentially means to defer meeting many of one's neighbors until spring.

The casualness of the encounters also means that the quality of the contact is somewhat superficial; nothing very personal or complex is likely to be shared while carrying in the groceries or when having to leave any second to rescue a toddler in distress.

The neighborhood women's groups provided a chance to get to know each other better and to talk more in depth about "whatever is important to you." Over a period of two years two different groups have existed. The first group was begun when the first author invited five neighborhood women to her home to discuss the idea of a group, and all decided to give it a try. At the formation of the second group, all interested women on the street were invited to participate; ten chose to do so. In both cases the women wanted a chance to talk about things of importance that they otherwise had little opportunity to pursue; to have two hours of adult conversation uninterrupted by children's needs, which was a rarity for them; and to do these things with the women whom they saw every day on their street, so that the closeness they hoped might develop in such a group would contribute to a sense of community.

We were aware that the Women's Center was addressing similar concerns for women throughout the county, but we still saw a need for such groups to be organized on a neighborhood level. The Women's Center was helpful and supportive of us in this intent.

The neighborhood women's groups met different needs for each person. At the very least, a few neighbors got to know each other better than they would have otherwise, at least in that short a time period. Some women received important support and understanding at difficult times in their lives. For others, the discussions stimulated and crystallized a lot of thinking. There were no observable negative effects from the groups and many very positive ones, both from the standpoint of personal growth and of a sense of community.

BABYSITTING CO-OP

There often seemed to be a shortage of teenage sitters in Columbia, and finding a daytime sitter during the school year was an especially difficult task. While the Columbia Association operated, hourly day care program was an excellent one, it was not always the best arrangement (and was no help at all for infants; the program cannot accept children under age 2). Economic considerations are also important considering the current rate of $1 per hour for teenage sitters and $1.25 per hour at hourly day care. Columbia provided many recreational, educational, and volunteer opportunities from which the unemployed parent can especially benefit, but only if there is suitable child care. And of course there were other daytime obligations, such as doctor's appointments, etc., to be met. Certainly it was the rare resident who had nearby relatives to help out. Cooperative babysitting was one way to meet these needs.

The Meadows Babysitting Co-op membership was open to all residents of the Meadows townhouses (about 200 units on 4 streets) at no cost. On entering the co-op a person received 45 pieces of scrip, each good for 30 minutes of babysitting (which must be returned on leaving the co-op), a list of all the other members, and a set of co-op rules. Each member made her/his own arrangements for a sitter by calling members on the list. Members were free to refuse any specific "sit" request or to specify their interest in sitting only during the day, only in evenings, etc. Whether members relied solely on the co-op for meeting child care needs or used it in addition to paid sitters, relatives, or friends, the co-op was helpful to a large number of residents.

Rules for Children

On our CDS there were definite but informal guidelines for appropriate behavior for children. For instance, any big toy—"Big Wheel," tricycle, etc.—left outside in the front yard was "fair game" for any child so long as it was returned near the yard it came from. There was also agreement that the little children were not to go beyond a certain distance from the houses. Because of the agreement on certain rules, any adult could and did intervene when a child violated one.

Conclusions

The above activities are certainly not innovative; moreover, they are but a subsample of those found in many communities. Their importance lies in that all of them involved the same small group of people and some were purposefully designed to promote a feeling of community. Self reports suggest that such common neighborhood activities are highly valued. People who had been gone from the CDS for over a year often reported that they were still experiencing a loss of community from having moved. For many, the CDS was the first geographically based community that they had experienced as adults. Young, well-educated, and achievement-oriented, Columbians move often; yet the thesis of this paper is that a feeling of community can be developed despite resident turnover.

It is also important to note that we did none of the activities listed above as psychologists per se. We did them as residents, and we think the distinction is important. We have both formally consulted with other Columbia groups about psychological issues, but we feel that many important developmental opportunities are unfortunately overlooked by behavioral scientists in their immediate home settings that, in the long run, build communities and themselves as well.

16. A Psychologist Emerging as a Social Engineer[1]

DORIS WRIGHT

Many of us involved in new and renewing community development, believe strongly in the validity of the new town concept and challenge the notion that it has failed. Some extremely important lessons that have been learned about the process of building communities are what it is and how it works. It is in the context of such a process, that I find my work to be substantially fulfilling. My purpose here is to portray my role in the process as a whole, to describe the social and economic values created through the new town approach to building environments, and to convey the confidence I have about new towns and their contribution to the quality of life.

One of the central organizing concepts around which new towns are developed is that the needs of the people who live in them will be met. Herein lies the role for those

[1]I write this paper at a time when modern day U.S. new towns are under severe scrutiny. The Department of Housing and Urban Development (HUD) has announced its decision to discontinue assisting additional developers of new towns under the Housing and Urban Development Act of 1970. It seems that Congress had a vision for National Growth Policy, but the present administration and HUD, charged with its implementation, had little or no understanding of the validity of the new town concept and the process that could make the vision come true.

of us involved with human behavior. This in itself sets new towns apart from the housing developments that appeared in the 1950's and 1960's, or the shopping malls that popped up everywhere in later years. The primary motivation was for those housing developments to sell houses, the malls to sell space, and both to make big profits. The social concerns of people were not considered by the developers, and they did not pretend to build complete living environments.

It was in the early 1960's that I began to rebel. For years as a psychologist, I worked with young people, listening to their problems and to those of their families. Troubled youth came and went, but new ones always took their place, with the same frustrations, hang-ups, and unsolved problems as those who came before them. Counseling and teaching no longer seemed relevant, and neither was directed at the causes. I realized that the problems related continually to environmental and social issues. I began to conceptualize prevention rather than treatment as a better approach. It seemed so logical, why was it so hard for so many people to understand? The systems had to change. They had to respond to human need in different ways and with different attitudes toward preventing mental and physical breakdown. Resources must be spent to prevent crises, not treat them.

LAUNCHING A NEW CAREER

It was at this point in my own growth and development that I made the decision to change careers and I look on the experiences that followed as my "postgraduate study" in the social engineering facet of urban planning. To change careers at 40 seemed pretty ridiculous for anyone, but for a woman to plunge into one that belongs to men was absolutely insane. We should begin with how my training in psychology fits into urban planning. Only good psychology, the best laid plans, and a lot of luck could make the breakthrough.

I used every skill I could muster in the early 1960's to convince Harold Edelston, Executive Director of the Health and Welfare Council of the Baltimore Area, to hire me as a planner and place me in Baltimore County (the days when Spiro T. Agnew was County Executive). For three years I was Director of the Baltimore County Health and Welfare Council, Youth Commission and Commission on Aging. The experience provided the opportunity to understand the systems and conceive ideas about how a community and its institutions should work for people. I began to understand their constraints, which were usually financial, time, personnel, or system structure. Any or all of them kept "business as usual" and made real change hard to accomplish.

About this time, when I was making a conscious effort to change some of the programs within the systems that served people in Baltimore County, the Rouse Company announced its plans for a new town. A "balanced" community, James Rouse called it. That word intrigued me. What did the developer mean by "balanced?" My own interpretation was that it would be a community in which all socioeconomic levels and ages of people could live, and one in which the opportunities would be there that are necessary to fulfill their lives: housing choices, jobs, shopping, learning opportunities, recreation, transportation, health and social services, spiritual relationships, and anything human beings need to assist them in meeting their everyday needs and achieving their personal and family goals.

If, indeed, this was the developer's intent, it seemed to me to be a modern day miracle. I saw it as an opportunity for social change that could have long lasting effects on the lives of people and I set out to find a way to participate. My goal, then as it is now, was to prevent social breakdown and enhance the quality of life. Let me say, I was naive and had much to learn. However, some of the events that have taken place, the results of my efforts, and the importance that psychology has played in my work may be enlightening.

Three periods in my second career have been crucially important, each with its own set of experiences: one year as Assistant Manager of the Columbia Association in charge of Human Resources in Columbia, Maryland; almost three years with the Greater Hartford Process as social/institutional planner; and nearly two years as President of REP Associates, a research, evaluation, and planning firm.

The year with the Columbia Association made certain things evident. First, it was clear that even developers who have a vision about the quality of life do not grasp easily the real values that can be created by comprehensive social planning. They seldom see social planning as an equal part of the planning process—equal, that is, to the physical and economic components. Second, it was apparent that residents in new towns brought their problems and expectations with them. Their expectations that things would be better, more beautiful, more fun, more convenient, and that coping with life would be easier were often not realized. Third, I realized that building a beautiful environment does not change automatically the social systems that must respond to human problems.

These issues had important implications for me and for the tasks ahead. I soon learned that my professional jargon was a liability and I better learn the language of the developer very fast. I knew I had to understand the work of the physical planner, know the economic issues, and be able to insert my social concerns into the planning process in those terms. This took quite some time to grasp.

SOCIAL PROBLEMS OF THE NEW TOWN

The social problems in the early stages of the new town became clear. Youth were attracted from all over the region; runaways found their way to Columbia; and misuse of drugs was a growing concern. Good child care and after school recreation programs encouraged single-parent families to move in. Expectations for services were higher than what could be delivered in the early stages. Families were overextended financially because they bought homes that were too expensive for them. Socioeconomic integration required adjustments and understanding. Health services were difficult to get. Engaging the existing agencies and institutions in program planning after Columbia was underway caused dissension between Columbia and Howard County agencies that must service the new town.

These increasing and immediate social issues began to beg the broader questions with which we were concerned initially: Can we make a community work better? How can the economic viability of a comprehensive social planning effort be proved? How can roles for youth and for elderly be built into the fabric of community life? How can priorities be changed to channel resources into new programs that prevent mental and physical breakdown rather than those that just treat them? What can be learned from the emerging new town that can be applied in old towns?

For Columbia, the answer came in a piecemeal fashion. Problems were identified as new programs were initiated and a town began to emerge. Many of the problems became opportunities for me as a social planner. For example, in the low-income housing units, many indicators, such as fear, vandalism, carelessness, and people behind in their rent, pointed to the need for resident managers. Resident managers seemed very expensive to the housing management, and no one understood the long term economic value, to say nothing of the human value, they could bring. However, many months later—months of costly experiences—the resident manager system was established. A person was there who understood those living in the community; there to hear the problems when the rent could not be paid, to assist people in finding jobs, to help them understand the opportunities in the new town; there to encourage flowers to be planted in the yards, to fix a drippy faucet with a part instead of a whole new faucet, and there to watch that vandalism was controlled. Two years after resident managers were installed, vandalism was reduced significantly, costs for renovating after people moved went from as much as $1,500 to $200 per unit, yards were kept up, homes were in good repair by the renters, and the late rents were reduced by 47 percent. Many thousands of dollars have been saved and human life has been maximized because of just one social concept that was initiated. It is a very good demonstration of the community arithmetic of social planning. The developer understands these kinds of costs and benefits. A footnote to this is that the Howard County Community College in Columbia now has a comprehensive two year course in housing management which is one of the few in the nation.

Some problems were more serious than others and people suffered severely before the opportunity for change was identified, as the following experience with a neighborhood food outlet shows. The idea of making a neighborhood store a community space had been a concept we had discussed from time to time. It seemed realistic to think that the old general store with men sitting around the pot belly stove, and the drug store that was the teenage hangout of the 1940's, could be replaced by something other than noncommercial community facilities that were expensive to build and to operate. We proposed such a place at the neighborhood level that first year: a place where the community was actively part of the commercial activity that would include a coffee house, arts and crafts place, with drama and music. It was not, however, until a neighborhood quick food store, victimized by many robberies, was in financial trouble and had to close the door, that the developer saw an opportunity to try something different. Two years later, a place called "Mrs. Z's" took the place of that neighborhood store. It was clearly an advantage to the developer to have a paying tenant who provided both community activities and a contribution to the quality of life. Mrs. Z's is a place where people come to talk, sing, eat, buy crafts and homemade bread, or barter with something they have for something from Mrs. Z's. It is Columbia at its best.

Certain interest groups such as the elderly, youth, or children inspire special kinds of planning efforts. Planning for children was in the form of a comprehensive child development center. It must be said that planning for other people's children requires skill in dealing with people. I do not want to dwell here on the scenario relative to child care that took place that first year. It would be well to point out, however, that my assumptions about developing a system of child care and development for a community have changed, and I would not begin as we did in Columbia. The assumption there was that a very good comprehensive early childhood development program would be a marketing feature for the new town, and that it was. Moșt everyone with small children "bought a child care program" when they bought their house and whether or not they needed or could afford it, they put their child in it. Families accepted, as a way of life, that children from three to five belonged in that center. However, conflicts arose in the center and in the homes. Tracing them, it was clear that many of the families where the mother did not work could not afford the child care center and finances became difficult. Since then, I have had new experiences that have contributed to the way I now think and plan for child care and development.

In the conceptual stages of planning for Columbia a policy decision was made to do no special planning for elderly people. James Rouse believed they should be integrated into the community and that planning separately for them would segregate them. It soon became apparent, however, that special considerations for older people must be made if they were to live and participate in community life there. Such things as planning for housing choices, transportation, recreational opportunities, and walkways, all of which are barrier free and accessible to older people, began to attract my attention. It became clearly evident that physically limited people, whether old or young, could not have access to many of the activities and much of the beauty of Columbia. Since then I have encouraged barrier free design in every project in which I have become involved.[2]

It seemed particularly difficult to plan effectively for teenagers. The teenage population was a community-wide issue in Columbia as in every new and old town in the country. Believing it to be an extremely crucial group within our society, I was determined to try to find some answers. It was not something that I accomplished the first year in Columbia. But as I studied planned communities here and abroad, some patterns began to emerge that provided me with some criteria for planning for youth.

In Denmark, England, and Holland, I found that ethnic groups among teenagers tend to segregate for recreational and cultural activities. Music was the one most important factor in determining who participated in any particular teenage center or program. Columbia's experiences have been similar. Their three youth centers became distinctly different racially and in terms of age groups participating. Columbia tried to fully integrate these youth centers, but with little success.

In my study of youth centers, I was able to make these observations.

—Youth Centers, operated by towns or adult organizations, with youth advisory panels, were more successful than those centers operated by the youth themselves.
—Large youth centers, with a variety of rooms designated for particular activities and interests, had a larger degree of success than centers with only general use space.

[2] *Cost of Barrier Free Design,* by Doris Wright, 1975 (unpublished, available from author).

—Commercial centers were extremely successful from a participation standpoint as well as being economically sound.

There are some interesting models that exemplify these observations. For example, in Stevenage, England it was proved that youth do not like to be responsible for the administrative tasks of their own leisure activities. (This is no different than adults. Most of us do not want all the work that goes along with planning and implementing leisure opportunities). Their large, centrally located teenage center was less than successful at first when the youth ran the programs and the center itself. Three years later, the Board of Education took it over and successfully operated it, with youth advisory committees. That center, as with other successful large ones that I visited, had ethnic and cultural groups "doing their thing" separately. One room was particularly interesting to observe. They had two groups that met in the same room, each three nights a week. One was a passive "hippie" type that sat on cushions and heard soft music. The other group, "the black jackets," had card tables with checkered tablecloths and loud rock. Each had its own instant decor and one could hardly believe it was the same room.

Although youth did not operate their own centers, I found throughout Europe that they did organize and operate programs for others. In Stevenage, they ran programs for elderly people. In Amsterdam they worked with the child care programs, and in Copehagen I found them operating gardening classes for children and woodworking classes for all ages. In all of the areas, as Columbia has found in their Mall, commercial centers with billiards, slot machines, and coin-operated games are popular and economically successful.

In planning for young people in Columbia, some things have proved to work out. Jobs for youth were part of Columbia from the first day anyone moved in. Employment opportunities for every teenager who wanted to work was a goal for all of us who were planning and implementing programs. It is a goal that has continued and one that has been reasonably met. Thousands of youth came to the plaza in Columbia in the summer, which in itself was a challenge. Over the years, new answers have been found, and summer activities have been developed that involve the youth as well as entertain them. Columbia has done a great deal to accept teenagers as human beings, as assets and not liabilities. This is a difficult concept for many to accept and implement. In most communities we have not found ways to build in contributing roles for our young people. Without such opportunities, can we expect positive behavior?

APPLYING LEARNINGS TO EXISTING COMMUNITIES

I left the Columbia Association to join the staff of the American City Corporation and had a major role in their effort to apply the Columbia process to old cities. Their first project was in the Greater Hartford Region. The Greater Hartford process, as it became known, was my most valuable learning experience. A basic concept was that social, physical, and economic planning were all part of one process. Developers have long understood the need for physical and economic plans, but the need for social planning was questionable. Hartford process accepted, and over time, understood its importance to the economic base of a community and to the quality of life. The lack of understanding of social planning, its economic and human value, has been greatly responsible for the lack of commitment of time and dollars to the social needs of our communities. A developer or city official finds it difficult to invest large sums of money for something he does not understand will give a substantial return.

Being part of a planning team that was to use the Columbia process on an existing region was an exciting prospect; describing the tasks of a social planning and development component of that process was a welcome challenge; and using that process to design new life support systems was the opportunity I had been looking for.

Hartford process lived up to its expectations. A description of the Hartford work is contained in the report "Social Institutional Development," Greater Hartford Process Inc., Hartford, Connecticut. It focused on systems and not fragmented elements of the systems which Columbia was forced to do. As a social planner, I was considered an equal part of the team. I developed a social/institutional planning and development process that worked over time, and my design for a new social services delivery system was accepted and implemented. The process focused on ways to bring about social change, new ways to administer and finance life support systems, and new attitudes toward funding preventive programs rather than remedial ones. That process became an important product for me. When I organized my own firm, it is that process of social engineering on which I base my ability to bring about appropriate social change in new and renewing communities.

Being in charge of my own firm has provided me with varied opportunities to put into action what I have learned. We are involved in all aspects of planning with public and private sectors, managing the development process, in engaging the community around a conceptual plan, instituting social/institutional plans for a new town, and preparing social impact studies; all aimed at enhancing the quality of life.

The business is growing and the reason has become increasingly apparent. A new demand of a liaison between a public or private developer and the people and institutions of a community is emerging. Interpreting the developer's plan to the community and the community's needs to the developer is a role I have found myself accepting increasingly, and one I find very rewarding. The responsibility ranges from convincing the residents of a locality to accept a group home for youth to accepting the development of a whole community; from convincing developers to be concerned about safety across a railroad to accepting the idea of building a whole community that is as concerned about maximizing human values as they are with developing an esthetically pleasing environment or increasing economic value. I see this emerging role as a potential for encouraging public and private partnerships that can indeed bring about significant social change and enhance the quality of life.

Only time will tell if I have made a difference. Psychology, common sense, and fundamental knowledge of planning and development techniques are the critical ingredients in the work I am doing.

Section IV

POINT-COUNTERPOINT

17. Introduction

The contributions to this section speak for themselves. They are part of a tradition that has already been established within the Community Psychology Series of providing a concluding section of point-counterpoint. In it, several views are provided that are relevant to what has gone before in the issue.

In this section, Roland Warren, a well-known community sociologist; John Levering, formerly on the development staff for Columbia and its first manager; and the editor of this issue speak in various ways to the implications of new community development for the physical, social, and psychological well-being of large numbers of people.

The final commentaries must, of course, be provided by you, the reader.

18. Some Observations on the Columbia Experience

ROLAND L. WARREN

The articles in this volume present an embarrassment of riches to the would-be commentator. I found myself reacting to one point or another on nearly every page, but space limitations make a detailed commentary on each point unwise. My observations will therefore have to be somewhat more general, thus losing some of the taste and smell of the rich data imparted by the different authors.

Numerous writings point to the goals and aspirations of the new town movement, and they need not be repeated here. What seems to be most basic is that new towns presumably constitute an opportunity to "start from scratch," to build a new community with some idea of how the parts can fit meaningfully together and with some plans for control.

There are, of course, other proposed solutions to uncontrolled and undirected urban growth, and other ways of trying to deal creatively and aggressively with alternatives to the troubled urban industrial communities. Perhaps the most creative but the least "relevant" to the everyday world is the building of imaginative utopias after a pattern that reaches back to Plato's *Republic* and includes such idealistic works as Bacon's *New Atlantis,* More's *Utopia,* and Butler's *Erewhon.* Though challenging to the imagination, none of these constitutes a blue-print for action, and even such latter-day utopias as Skinner's *Walden Two* become transmuted when the attempt is made to use them as blueprints for actual communities.

The second alternative to conventional city growth patterns is an attempt to set up actual experimental communities, which, like the utopias, differ markedly from the main culture, and whose reason for being is to offer drastic alternatives to the existing pattern, to find a "new way" by people who are so convinced of its necessity that they are willing to pull up stakes, sever their ties from the larger society, and undergo the hardships and discipline of founding a new society, however small—and in most instances, fleeting.

New towns, likewise, are an attempt to start all over, to build communities closer to the ideal. But they differ from utopias and experimental communities in the important respect that they do not reject modern culture. Rather, they attempt to apply modern planning and technology to the building of relevant, livable communities, whose quality of life—that fleeting concept—will be higher than that of the surrounding communities which have experienced unplanned growth. As such, they have offered an exciting prospect for launching out in new directions as well as accommodating population growth by draining off the huge expected increase in the urban population in the next decades.

A few years ago, there was a widespread sense that new towns would be an important, if not dominant, feature of the future social and physical landscape. In retrospect, the hopes which supported the wave of enthusiasm for new towns appear to have been exaggerated. William Alonso (1970) probably did more than any other single analyst to keep the bubble of expectations from growing too big. He pointed to the National Committee on Urban Growth Policy's recommendation that before the year 2000, 100 new towns of at least 100,000 people and 10 new cities of at least 1 million be built to accommodate the expected urban growth of 100 million by the end of the century. Taking these rather enthusiastic figures at face value, however, he asserted that "The year 2000 would see only 7 percent of the 300 million population residing in these new settlements, with 80 percent of the foreseen growth taking place in existing areas."

But with the retrenchment begun in the Nixon administration and continued through the present, there are few people around who would accept as realistic the recommendation of the National Committee on Urban Growth Policy. Nevertheless, sooner or later there will be a new wave of new towns, and meantime, the lessons to be learned from the experience so far have implications for the older, crescive communities as well.

What lessons are to be drawn from the series of articles in this volume describing various aspects of Columbia in some detail? Perhaps the most surprising aspect of these reports is the impression they give of being so much like reports from crescive communities. It is difficult to select aspects of the experience which are determined substantially by the specific nature of Columbia as a new town. But a few aspects of the structure of Columbia are different from most communities and appear to have a direct bearing on the events and sequences reported so far.

First, in the presence of the developer and his staff, and of the Columbia Association, there was a central rubric with a somewhat broader purview than that of most city governments. There was, perhaps, more of a sense of being responsible for the whole "community" rather than just for a city government. There was some central provision for physical facilities and for at least modest support of new social ventures. There was apparently more of a sense of the clear need and mandate for what Klein calls "institutional development," based on the fact that it was a new town, that there were mechanisms for development, and that gradually, a whole institutional structure needed to be built. Indeed, the chance to plan the structure was part of the rationale for Columbia to begin with.

Last, there was, as Klein has described it, a concentration of behavioral scientists who had either been brought there in connection with one or another project or who had moved there. How much larger this concentration was than might be found in Newton or Scarsdale or Grosse Point, is of course open to question.

There may be other special characteristics of Columbia as a new town for which a claim could be made that they contributed specifically to the developments recounted in the foregoing articles. It would be especially instructive if there were noteworthy instances for which a stronger case could be made that they arose out of the activities of behavioral scientists or were a more or less planned result of the new town developmental sequence.

Perhaps the development which received the most enthusiastic and repeated mention by the writers is the Grassroots organization. Its inception out of a coalition in response to the initiative of a number of counter-culture youth was hardly unique, and Feinstein aptly designates it as "one of hundreds of peer-style help centers started in the late 1960's and early 1970's . . ." It is certainly an interesting organization; but again there seems to be nothing about it which indicates that its development was contingent upon a new town setting or upon the special intervention of behavioral scientists. Parenthetically, one can but blink in amazement at the observation, made now at the turn of the last quarter of the twentieth century, that "Grassroots is an alternative service by virtue of its policy of accepting all who come, serving them promptly, keeping them out of trouble-fraught official hands such as the police whenever possible, charging no fees, and referring them, when the problem is beyond the agency's competence, to another agency with more specific or intensive skills . . . Appointments are not required, there are no delays due to complex intake procedures, there is no waiting list, services are provided at unusual hours, and staff can go to the scene of a mental health emergency to do crisis intervention work." One can but ask in stupefaction: If these characteristics of an alternative institution are so exceptional, then what are Americans getting for their multi-billion dollar investment in social and mental health services?

In planned communities, as in other planned enterprises, there is an expected slippage between the cup and the lip. That slippage is illustrated by many points made in these articles, and has been dealt with more expressly in Richard Brooks' (1974) interesting volume on Columbia.

The slippage is to be expected for a number of reasons. There are terrific constraints on building a new community from scratch and having it turn out according to plan. Probably the most important constraint is the most obvious one: People are going to occupy those fine new houses, and they are going to bring with them their own hopes, desires, prejudices, potentialities, and limitations. The developer may truly have a "vision splendid" of the kind of social existence that will be realized there, but he cannot change people's desires or life-styles to any great extent. The attempt to impose his own social blueprint for the community onto the residents in any forceful way is both repugnant and, in any case, virtually impossible. Yet, if the plan is to remain inviolate in its implementation, it can only occur through some mixture of coercion and willing assent. The developer may wish the residents to remain in the community for their recreation, and they may prefer to drive miles away. He may prefer that a high proportion of people who live there also gain their livelihood from employment by local enterprises, but it may not be possible to attract the proper balance and number of enterprises, and, in any case, an uncontrolled number of workers may prefer for any number of perfectly compelling reasons to commute somewhere else. He may prefer that they use public transportation rather than their automobiles for shopping, and they will do substantially as they please. He may prefer that the local neighborhood become an important area for meaningful social participation, and they may or may not want to invest their leisure time in visiting with neighbors, preferring again, to drive miles away to people whom they choose to associate with on some other basis than that they bought a house on the same street.

A second constraint is that it is difficult if not impossible to create "community." The design of the residential pattern may favor or disfavor certain types of social activity, and it is possible through deliberate organizational efforts to stimulate greater social interaction among people who live close to each other. But people have an obdurate way of forming their own social ties, of building, or refusing to build, their own web of social relationships, their own set of feelings about the locality, their own participation patterns, their own emphasis on commonalities or differences in values, interests, and life-styles. Formal organizational efforts can accomplish specific objectives in many cases, but their influence on setting the "tone" of the community is probably much less than the natural, self-generating, informal set of feelings and relationships on which community in any other than a purely ecological sense, depends.

A third constraint is that the larger society cannot be "kept out" of the new community. The original plan for Columbia's school system suffered heavy attrition because of the fact that it was controlled not by Columbia but by Howard County. Likewise, Columbia cannot control industrial development outside its own borders, and the developments that have occurred have had important consequences for Columbia itself. The national housing market and the interest rate, both products of the national economy, have had a huge effect on the growth of Columbia. The federal government's withdrawal from support of new low-income housing has altered the planned balance of income groups in Columbia. Fashions, behavior patterns, products, social inventions, and life styles of Columbia's residents are affected constantly by the daily injection of stimuli from the larger society through the media. This is just another way of saying that

Columbia, as a new town, is *not* an experimental utopian community deliberately shut off from the rest of society. It is an open community in an open society, and the boundaries of ownership and control are highly permeable. In this sense, Columbia is but another stage, slightly different in construction, on which the drama of American society is enacted locally by American people. With all its blemishes, as well as its many beautiful aspects, American society is in Columbia just as much as it is in Washington or Baltimore. The local differences are highly important, but they can easily be exaggerated.

Would it be possible, within the limitations of a democratic society, to exert more formal control in order that at least some of the initial plans might suffer less attrition? Certainly, the federal government might take much more aggressive action to support them. Conceivably, new town development could occur under governmental, rather than private profit, auspices. Legislation could provide for inducements for industries to locate in new towns, thus making more feasible the elimination or drastic reduction in commuting for employment. Priority in the availability of residences could be given to those who have firm commitments for employment in the new town. All of these things are done in the British new towns system, whose success has been more notable than new towns in this country. But they call for a much greater commitment to the idea of new towns than seems to be present in the present administration or, for that matter, among American voters.

Columbia has been "researched to death," and rightly so. Most of the research has been confined to Columbia and has not provided a systematic basis for comparison with other settings. Part of the difficulty in designing such research is that Columbia has few counterparts in other new communities in the United States. One notable exception to the lack of comparative research designs is that of a research project at the University of North Carolina, which included Columbia in its study of 17 new communities and 19 comparison communities (Burby & Weiss, 1976). The study found that new communities showed a higher rating on most indicators of satisfaction with the immediate neighborhood and with the overall community although the differences were very small. The new communities had a clear advantage in the area of recreation facilities. One conclusion the researchers draw, however, is that greater results on the indicators they used might be obtained through smaller planned unit developments than through an equivalent investment in large planned communities.

But the definitive word is not yet in, either on Columbia or new towns in general, or even on the findings and implications of the study just cited. When it is written, there is little room for doubt that it will contain new learnings, not only about the benefits and costs of new towns, but about ways of helping improve the quality of life which will be useful to the crescive communities as well.

One can but laud the audacity as well as the broad social concern and purpose shown by the developer, James W. Rouse (whose own comments in this volume I have not seen as this is written), in undertaking a project of this economic magnitude and social audacity and with the degree of human concern which went into it from the outset. In these days when one feels a pathetic lack of federal leadership with respect to urban policy and urban problems, the Columbia effort, with all its imperfections, accomplishments, fulfillments, and expectations, stands out as one of the most promising and energetic developments in the whole field of urban planning. That it could be brought off at all under today's conditions is in itself a remarkable feat. It will surely be a basis for "doing it better" the next time the spotlight of public interest and support swings around to the new town concept. And part of the reason we can hope to build on a more sophisticated foundation of experience and knowledge is represented by the papers of this volume, which in turn reflect a concern for evaluation and feedback into the continuous process of coping with the problems of over 200 million people in an urban industrialized society.

REFERENCES

Alonso, W. The mirage of new towns. *The Public Interest,* Spring, 1970.

Brooks, R. O. *New towns and communal values: a case study of Columbia, Maryland.* New York: Praeger, 1974.

Burby, R. J. III & Weiss, S. F., et al. *New communities U.S.A.* Lexington, Mass.: Lexington Books 1976.

19. *Evaluation of a New Town—Relative to What?*

JOHN LEVERING

The commitment to build a new city would seem to represent one of the noblest of human aspirations. For ages people in the city have waged the necessary and difficult struggle of living together in relative safety and with at least minimal satisfaction of human needs. The city has been the seed bed and nurturing place of political process, social systems, dialogue, meeting, culture, art, learning, education. Yet we live in an age that witnesses the near collapse of the city as even a habitable human environment.

So the new city is at its best a new and renewed vision of the city as it might be. The purpose of new city is to recapture that which is enriching and enlivening about city life, and to restore it to a more human scale and build in greater harmony with nature. A place large enough for a creative output from its critical mass, yet so ordered that a person might live with the individual dignity and natural contact with others that together make community.

Columbia emerged from such impulses. I moved here to work in its development. I now have a new career, yet still live and work here. Often I am asked (simply because I live here, sometimes because of what I have done here): "How's Columbia doing?" "Has it met your expectations?" "Do you really like living there?" "Has it worked out the way it was planned?" Most such questions I answer affirmatively. Most of the time I have felt that I have not responded fully; that my response was not fully understood; that the questioner did not know the questions.

I think there is very little genuine understanding of Columbia, of whether it is a success or a failure, or many of both. This is deeply troubling. Columbia needs to be better understood by its citizens for they are shaping it, changing it every day based on their perceptions and responses; and by its neighbors and by the county of which it is a part; and by developers, by governmental policy makers, by social scientists, and by planners. I do not suppose I "understand" Columbia either. I do think I see at least a part of the difficulty in perceiving more clearly its progress and meaning.

It is the wish to make simple and neat, something that is very complex and elusive. It is the recurring temptation to plan, develop, administer, study a new town as if it were some kind of discrete, insular event. There is even a pseudo-scientific kind of language, a "research" attitude that is applied as if a new town could be isolated and studied like some kind of sterile culture. My point is simply that the truth is precisely the opposite. The "culture" is thoroughly contaminated (if I may use that word without negative connotation).

We will never build a new town successfully, or formulate a new town policy, or abandon a new town policy for the right reasons, or do anything else about it correctly if we cannot begin by understanding what a new town is.

A part of the understanding must be that a new town is part of the larger whole. A new town exists entirely intermingled with its larger context. Context means neighbors, political subdivision, state, and nation; context also means society, culture, economics, technology, mores, etc.

Building a new town is a long-term undertaking. It is planned, begun, developed, and lived in over time. The new town and its context changes so rapidly that the term "future shock" coined by Toffler applies here.

Columbia was formed in concept in 1962. The planners involved were mostly Jim Rouse, President of the Howard Research and Development Corporation Company and the Rouse Company, Bill Finley, Project Director for Columbia, and Mort Hoppenfeld, Director of Planning and Design. The land was acquired mostly in 1963; its initial comprehensive plan presented in October 1964; zoning obtained in 1965; and initial development financing closed in December 1965. It was five years before the first resident moved into an apartment in June 1967. The scheduled development period was fifteen years, until 1982.

The planners began with farm land and planned for a completed city. They sought to design a physical environment and social systems that would work for that city. At the end of 1974, some 37,000 people live here and it is not yet the "new city" it is intended to be. It is something to keep in mind before we pass final judgment on whether or not it has worked.

In 1962 based on their opposition to urbanization, apartment zoning, and such, Howard County residents elected their first Republican County Commissioners in many years. Yet in 1965 that government approved the New Town District zoning. Then a new charter form of government was introduced to the County. A Democratic executive and a majority Democratic council was elected in 1966. It was generally positive in attitude toward Columbia's development. In 1970 another election placed in office a majority of County residents strongly reactionary, if not outright opposed to Columbia. In the Wallace/McGovern primary some issues were made startlingly clear. Every polling place in the County gave a majority to Wallace, except in Columbia. When Columbia went 8–1 for McGovern, he carried the County.

In late 1974 as this is written, the local news is the virtual domination of the County Council by Columbia-based men and women. It is worth remembering that the County is the authority for planning and zoning; that Columbia has county schools, police, fire protection, water, sewer, roads, etc. It exists in a larger context and that context has changed dramatically and often since 1962.

Zoning and development plans do not get processed as expeditiously in the County as they used to. It could be a mistake to think that the Columbia residents who are county council members will change that. Participation in the county government is one of the ways the residents of Columbia will be taking charge of the remaining development of their own city.

Every facet of life in Columbia is affected by these things, but it is not so clear just what the effects are. Columbia is not maintaining its planned pace of development. This is a crucial factor. In other places it has already been fatal to the developers' and to the residents' expectations. The political structure in the County has been a factor as have federal policy, the new consumerism, changing mores, the spiral up in inflation, and the spiral down in the stock market.

One of Columbia's earliest and most important objectives was the provision of a wide economic range of choices in housing and broad economic integration among its residents. One brief example may be illustrative of the experience to date. The developer in a joint venture built 300 high quality, three-bedroom townhouses. They were offered for sale at $14,500 to $17,500 in fee. Many people of moderate means were among the purchasers. In recent months, these houses have brought upwards of $35,000 at resale. They are no longer accessible for people with moderate to lower incomes.

In 1972 the Department of Housing and Urban Development froze substantially all subsidy, rent supplement, and related housing programs. Since 1967 construction cost indices have nearly doubled with no end or slowdown in sight. Mortgage interest rates have long since reached legal limits, if money is available at all. Under these conditions, there is no way Columbia will meet its targets in lower cost housing or economic integration. In this Columbia has failed, but relative to what?

Columbia began with many clearcut social objectives. Many have been achieved; many have not. The planners had, for example, many hopeful images about a creative role for teenagers in the new city. They planned on the basis of their experience, the world as they saw it in 1963–64, their best looks into the future. In 1963–64 most Americans had heard little about hard rock or of counter-cultures. There was little intimation of the coming revulsion over Vietnam and the anti-war protests. The fall of 1964 saw the first serious confrontations on the Berkeley Campus. Few could have guessed at events to come from there, to Kent State in 1970, to the still different mood of today.

Has Columbia "worked" for young people? How does one even shape the question? In this area, like many others in the social arena, we are at least dealing with an ongoing process. Low-cost housing is pretty much out of the reach of developers and local citizens today. It is not the same with people. Successes, failures, and learnings continue. New ideas are tried, old ways discarded, some old ones are tried again in new forms. Success and failure seem hardly even relevant words. Certainly the world of young people does not look like anything anyone might have planned 10 years ago. But in Columbia people are engaging the issues in a myriad of ways: some solidly based in established institutions, some through entirely new agencies evolved from grassroots, self-help efforts.[1]

Columbia was strongly shaped as an environment to be supportive of the nuclear family. What does one say about that in today's world of alternative life styles, communal

[1]One of the most significant is Grassroots, Inc., a "hot-line" crisis counseling service, initiated by teenagers, supported by the developer, professionals in the community and county and state agencies. Grassroots is discussed elsewhere in this monograph in an article by Allan Feinstein.

living, trial marriages; when less and less people want to marry or have children; when fewer and fewer presently married people want to stay that way? Sexual/family mores have changed. The pill entered widespread distribution in the mid-1960's. Legal and social barriers to birth control continue to break down. The planners could not anticipate the consequences of such fundamental changes. Columbia needs more places for singles to live and meet. This need was not foreseen. Howard County zoning is not tailored for singles, or communes or other alternative patterns. Yet, very substantial numbers of single people choose to live here. What conclusion does one draw?

Thirteen major Protestant denominations entered a commitment for cooperative ministry in 1966. The Protestant Church in America was riding the crest of the postwar wave. It has been downhill ever since. The religious institutions in Columbia have been affected fully and equally by the same broad, deepseated trends and forces. The church in Columbia does not match the blueprint. There is a Protestant team ministry without counterpart in America. There is genuine, deeply rooted interfaith sharing among Jews, Protestants, Catholics without precedent anywhere. And it is a sharing with solid tangible accomplishments in interfaith housing, facilities sharing, and programs.

It is not what was planned, but something beautiful and deeply significant is occurring. Without the vision and the plans none of it would have occurred. Has the dream been realized? I would say yes, because the dream itself has changed, because the dreaming goes on, because there are new dreamers and new doers.

Columbia has no clearer success than its breaking down of racial barriers in housing, in its shattering of old concepts by mingling housing prices and types in close proximity. It was an enormous accomplishment, but open housing does not seem to be "the" issue anymore. In 1963–64 the assassination of Martin Luther King was nearly 5 years away, and "Black is beautiful," and "Black Power" were not even a part of the language. There are racial problems today in Columbia. Some people work with them, some people hide from them.

There are "successes" in Columbia in new programs, new institutions that the planners did not initiate. The developers initiated some, helped others; some they probably are hardly even aware of. I really think Columbia is working as demonstrated by the following particulars:

There is a strong sense of community and identity.

There is an amazingly alive process of individual participation and involvement in endless ways. There is a sense of things being possible; boundless energy in experimentation.

There is a generally effective working relationship between the people and the developer, developer and county government, and people and government.

There is a strong industrial/commercial base. Howard County has been catapulted into the position of one of the most fiscally strong political subdivisions in America. It has literally all the economic resources it needs to meet the needs of all its people.

There has been sifted out of many trials and failures a solid core of creative new institutions and programs in secondary and higher education, health, religion, recreation, community self-help in many forms, in local communications media, and others. There is literally an overwhelming range of programs, groups, agencies, and activities started by County and Columbia citizens and new ones yet everyday.

So far it could be said that as a model Columbia might be counted a failure. Nobody's attempted a second Columbia. Perhaps it is well enough understood for developers to shy away from the commitment of resources, time, and costly involvement. One might hope that with a different kind of understanding this might change. It should be known that the product is ultimately a process, that it is possible to do something better and that the results are worth the cost and the risk. New town policy decisions need to be made with a clear understanding of what the subject is. That what Columbia is attempting is a new kind of city building. That what is required is possible, but that it is large and difficult and complex. Understanding of the size, scope, and complexity of such an undertaking is needed not so that we will be frightened or deterred, but so that we will not be naive, so that we can dream big enough, plan well enough, initiate processes open enough to make real and ongoing change.

It is too difficult to pass a final judgment on Columbia because it is not finished. In a sense, of course, no thriving city can ever be. But even in the more limited sense, Columbia is only ten years into the fifteen to twenty year period of its deliberate development. What will happen to Columbia even in the next year? The whole world is in turmoil. The entire worldwide economic systems are in disarray. Energy resources and inflation alone conjure up adequate uncertainties. How does a new city develop in such circumstances?

Columbia and other new towns must be looked at as they are if we are to learn anything from our experience to date. I believe the experience on balance has been extraordinarily good. I believe also, that any meaningful conclusions are dependent upon a very special, sophisticated examination. There must be recognition above all that a new city is not a thing apart, but a part of a series of larger wholes. A new city is really a myriad of processes moving in time.

20. Reflections on the Psychology of New Towns

DONALD C. KLEIN

As I review the contributions to this issue, I am struck by the realization that, even though, as Clapp points out, the city is man's "urban invention" dating back many thousands of years, we know very little about the fundamental dynamics that are unique to that invention. And yet, the articles underscore repeatedly the fact that however pleasing esthetically, however carefully designed structurally, however thoughtfully planned in terms of innovative political and social institutions, the comprehensive new town reflects basic social dilemmas inherent in all human settlements of our society.

The power of the utopian dream makes it easy to look for reasons in the larger society and there is, of course, no shortage of such reasons in the political and social history of the 1970's. Hanson's contribution does a surgeon's job of laying bare some of the absurdities of federal law and policy which have virtually ensured that in good times or bad, new towns could hardly prosper. McKissick's powerful dream of a multi-racial Soul City developed by black leadership remains juxtaposed in my mind with Toomer's resident's eye view of what delights and despairs transpire when such dreams are superimposed on a racist society.

Murrell's article is in some ways reflective of a core dilemma for community psychologists and other applied behavioral scientists who aspire to influence the quality of life in established as well as new communities. Much of what he was able to draw from in the design of NewCom represented a psychology of the individual, the group, the organization, and the interactions between groups, not the psychology of the community. Even the work of the ecological psychologists pertains to aggregates of people that number far less than even one neighborhood of most new towns. Psychology so far has failed to address itself significantly to the dynamics of the comprehensive community, despite the fact that it is one of humankind's oldest inventions. Even we community psychologists are constrained by our assumptions and methodologies that restrict us to investigations that can test hypotheses and yield quantifiable results. But the problems of designing entire communities cannot be encompassed by such inquiries. We are dealing, as Murrell recognized, with *macrosystems*—large, complex configurations of systems interacting with one another as they address themselves to areas of prime concern, such as incorporating newcomers, attending to the health needs of a population, providing services in support of family life, and going about the business of socializing and maturing entire new generations.

Probably at an even more fundamental level, we need to confront the issues raised by Rouse's strong concern for creating what he calls "a sense of place." It has been difficult for most community psychologists and other applied behavioral scientists to become greatly concerned about place. They are, for the most part, cosmopolitans who move along the flyways of academic and professional America, shifting repeatedly from location to location in pursuit of professional and academic fulfillment. They are part of the process whereby automobile and airplane have destroyed yesterday's sense of community based on geographic location. It is ironic in this regard that Murrell, the one community psychologist deeply involved in the design of a new community, found himself involved in planning a transitional community, one that would enable rural folk to make the giant step of leaving their accustomed, but no longer economically feasible, home place.

And yet it is clear to me from my experience with Columbia and from the contributions herein of community psychologists and others who found themselves engaged in the creation of new social institutions that Rouse is probably right; there is something compelling about finding oneself in a habitat which does, in fact, provide a strong sense of place. The articles describing the development of Grassroots, the Family Life Center, and the Women's Center all share the sense of excitement that comes from having played a significant part in the creation or improvement of one's home place. I think we community psychologists need to inquire further into this phenomenon.

There are at least three fundamental aspects of community which distinguish this human aggregate from all others, such as face to face groups and organizations. They include the special *sense of location,* physical and/or psychological, which is involved when humans (or other animals for that matter) stake out that piece of territory which represents their home place. The Youngs' paper reflects a fine sense of the significance of the home place and suggests just some of the ways in which informed participation can create supportive networks of interaction within cul-de-sacs and other clusters of dwelling units.

Another fundamental aspect of community long recognized by the political scientists and some sociologists has to do with *power* and the ways in which the various organized and unorganized components of community struggle over the allocation of scarce resources, such as land, money, prestige, and special technical skills. Even though Columbia remains a managed community in which the developer maintains a preeminent, though continuously shrinking influence, there are many indications that the emerging political process will not differ markedly from other moderately sized, well-educated communities (e.g., Eugene, Oregon or Berkeley, California). I remain hopeful that modern developments in communication technology (e.g., two-way closed circuit television) and behavioral technologies (e.g., approaches to conflict resolution and the design of communication systems based on immediate feedback) can be used to reduce the likelihood of unproductive conflict, polarization, and what I have termed the all too prevalent "community paranoia" that is endemic in many localities. Columbia's system of village boards and gathering places for even smaller neighborhood areas may provide the physical and institutional framework within which a creative political process can emerge. However, there is as yet no indication that the designers and implementers of the community are able to invest the money and time to encourage its emergence.

The third fundamental aspect of community has to do with *choice*. This quality of community was underscored both by Rouse and Murrell. A community to be viable in today's society must provide a variety of alternative pathways, both physical and social. Any attempt to restrict choice becomes in a sense not only a violation of freedom; it also represents an effort to institutionalize the life of the community, or even to make the community into institution. Individuals are positioned in organizations by virtue of their roles and responsibilities. They are positioned in communities primarily by virtue of their home place. Otherwise, to secure the various goods and services which they require throughout their lives they must move to other areas of the community and, most important, must make choices from among the various alternatives available to them. Part of the task of education for citizenship should be that of helping people learn how to discover the alternatives, how to choose from among them, and, when needed, how to create new ones. The process which the Rouse Company called institutional development that is reviewed by Wastie and Klein is inherently involved in determining both the choices to be made available by the developer of a new town and the mechanisms that hopefully will ensure that additional alternatives and choices will be crafted by residents as the need arises. I believe that the quality of life in any community is diminished seriously when significant numbers of people are deprived of viable choices within any aspects of their lives. Even the decision not to participate in the life of the community is experienced in a way that is fundamentaly different from a perceived inability to play a meaningful part.

The contributions to this issue suggest that new towns do have the capacity to create meaningful choices, partly because of the fact that they are developed on a large enough scale to warrant an investment in worthwhile alternatives. However, in the case of the material pertaining to Columbia a note of caution should be sounded. Columbia is an emerging new town. It is a *developing* community, not a developed one, and it seems as hard to predict what a new town will become when it is fully established and peopled as it is to forecast the nature of the adult from the character study of the ten-year-old. Part of the excitement of Columbia up to this time has been that it is a developing community. Early residents have found it easy to share the developer's dream and in some cases to become colleagues in the development process. Though not exactly undermanned in Barker's sense, the emerging new city does offer a myriad of opportunities for significant participation. Everyone feels in the same boat; everyone can share in the sense of creation. There is an informality and camaraderie that is reminiscent of the frontier settlement or of the Army barracks where barriers of education and experience have no function.

I sense that this youthful, innocent phase of Columbia's development is drawing to a close. Beyond a certain size, which I believe lies somewhere between 20,000 and 40,-

000 people, it is possible for relatively few residents to encompass in their daily lives most of the focii of excitement and concern that are current at any point in time. Cliques and continuing interest groups become increasingly closed to outsiders. The community's "management decisions" get made by an ever-shrinking proportion of the population. Areas, neighborhoods, and villages live with histories and reputations which affect the choices that can be made, opening certain options and closing others. The guiding dream of the original developer shrinks in comparison with the ever-present realities of dealing with conflicting needs and priorities of groups whose contacts with each other become less and less consensual.

In a sense this issue of the Community Psychology Series can only freeze for a moment the process of emergence of the new community. Ideally what is needed is a continuing participant-observation process whereby a team of applied behavioral scientists could pool from time to time the data they would be gathering from differing vantage points as the new town grew in size and complexity. Some of us at CoRAL II have considered making the services of that organization available for just such a process, perhaps on an annual basis. If, despite serious limitations of funding and staff, such a process is initiated, our findings may be publishable in a subsequent issue of this Series.

In the meanwhile, it is probably pertinent to ask what can psychologists offer new towns, especially if so little is known by the field about the psychology of community life? Let me begin by asserting that I now believe that psychologists know at least as much about community life as the physical designers, land use experts, road builders, and others who now make crucial decisions about the shape of new communities. There is no inherent wisdom in the highway engineer's training or experience that insures an optimal layout of the road network of a new town. I suspect that community psychologists charged with the design of the human services network would fall short of the ideal no more often than do the highway designers in their own sphere.

The contributions to this issue suggest ways in which psychology can be made relevant to new town development. A partial list might be:

1. the application of psychological knowledge to the design of the physical layout of the community (Murrell and Wright)
2. the participation in the process of preplanning the design of basic institutions (Wastie and Klein)
3. the involvement of citizens and developers' representatives alike in the process of identifying human needs and the design of ways to respond to them (Feinsten, Shoffeits, and Eberhardt)
4. in-depth studies of ways in which the physical and social design of the community impinges on significant subgroups (Karsk and Klein)
5. consultations and other interventions designed to help prevent or resolve intergroup conflicts (Toomer)
6. using educational methods from community development and humanistic psychology to foster community leadership emergence, support networks, and problem solving (Eberhardt, Feinstein, and Klein)
7. the creative use of self as citizen to foster support networks and meaningful interdependence among groups, e.g., at the neighborhood level (Youngs)

Are new towns working? Perhaps the question should be stated, "Would they work if our urban policy truly supported their development?" Levering's paper and Warren's remarks are instructive in this regard. The latter quotes one expert on new community development as expecting "slippage" between cup and lip in planned communities as in other planned enterprises. The former emphasizes how such a question must be qualified by considerations of changing societal contexts and a complex process whereby successes and failures of concept and design are sifted out over time.

One major study in the field compared 17 new communities (none fully developed) with a similar number of "significantly less planned conventional" communities (Burby and Weiss, 1976). The findings indicate that, according to the perceptions of residents and other informants, new communities are superior to conventional community growth in: (1) better land use planning and access to community facilities; (2) reduction in automobile travel; (3) superior recreational facilities; (4) enhanced community livability; and (5) improved living environments for low- and moderate-income households, blacks, and the elderly. However, community identity, satisfaction with family life and the community as a place to raise children, neighboring, and participation in community organizations "were not much different in new than in conventional communities [p. 9]."

I do not know what to make of the above findings. Perhaps the Yogas and psychoanalysts are right who say that inner peace does not depend on one's physical environment. However, I would prefer to keep the questions open and encourage my colleagues in community psychology to undertake in depth comparisons not only of respondents' satisfactions and perceptions but also of the ways in which they seek and find the answers to life's challenges within new towns and conventional locales.

REFERENCE

Burby, R.J., III & Weiss, S.F. *New communities U.S.A.* Lexington, Mass.: Lexington Books, 1976.